BEHIND THE SCENES WITH HOLLYWOOD'S MOST DARING ADVENTURE HERO!

This is the book that tells all, following Chuck from the bottom up; from his school days as a pushed-around "half-breed," to success as a karate instructor and tournament fighter, to taking Hollywood by storm as one of America's best-loved men of action.

Byron Coley's colorful and insightful biography gets into the inner workings of the man, and explains why he is so successful and one of our most important role models.

"Norris's capacity for steady hard work, matched with an almost legendary evenness of temper, elicits great loyalty and respect."

—*Moviegoer*

"Norris, you should know, is a nice, no-nonsense guy . . . and his fans have dutifully filed into drive-ins across the country to catch his act . . . Want a kick? Meet Chuck Norris!"

—*People*

CHUCK
NORRIS

BYRON COLEY

A ^{2}M communications ltd
production

ST. MARTIN'S PRESS
NEW YORK

CHUCK NORRIS
Copyright © 1986 by 2M Communications, Inc., and
Byron Coley

First printing/May 1986

ISBN: 0-523-90098-8
Can. ISBN: 0-523-90099-6

Photo research by Amanda Rubin

This book's for my parents and Lili.
They know why.

The author's grateful acknowledgment to James Truman for gracefully giving permission to quote from his extensive interview.

Special thanks to Richard Meltzer, Glenn Morrow, 2M, Valle Dwight, Tom Givan, Jimmy Johnson, David Greenberger, Robert Nedelkoff, the staffs of the Boston Public Library (Copley), the Lamont Library (Harvard), Movies Unlimited (Watertown), Sonic Youth (New York) and The Great Dull (Palos Verdes)

CHUCK NORRIS

1

In the far-flung future, the year 1985 will be remembered for all manner of portentous happenings: the world waited impatiently for Halley's Comet to arc visibly through the ether for the first time since Mark Twain breathed his last; our president petitioned to have the national debt ceiling raised to $3 trillion; Mick Jagger impregnated Jerry Hall for a second time; billions of fat-bottomed music fans sat glued to their television sets for seventeen marathon hours, in hopes that their time away from the kitchen would help to put meat on the bones of skeletal Ethiopians. Amidst all this brouhaha, a quiet Californian named Chuck Norris released three motion pictures. Before Mick and Jerry's offspring had gurgled its first, Norris was a major star.

Norris's first dozen movies took in something like $300 million. This is no mean testament to his popularity amongst what *The New York Times* calls "the unsophisticated public," but during 1985 a sizable portion of the more "sophisticated" public (the part that doesn't have to pony up five bucks per ticket to see his flicks) also began to recognize Norris's appeal. Film critics, once content to call him "America's favorite piece of driftwood," began falling all over themselves to find words that could adequately describe the stark minimalism of his style. One astute writer penned that Norris "has now fused the mythological dexterity of Bruce Lee with the equally mythological All-American gung-ho of John Wayne."

Sometime during the year, the man who'd previously been most often cited as one who'd "fought to the death with Bruce Lee" entered the mainstream of American pop culture the way a killer whale enters a wading pool: splash! His own films rode the very top of *Variety*'s box-office charts. Sylvester Stallone stole the story lines from two of Norris's Nam epics, pumped them full of steroids, and peddled them as *Rambo*. Where critics once said Norris looked like "a young Jimmy Carter," he was soon being described as "a craggy Robert Redford." His per-film fee approached the sums demanded by Clint Eastwood and Burt Reynolds (two shadows he's long been chasing). And all but the most liberal of newspapers wreathed him with garlands of praise. In fact, one of the few movie-related honchos who wasn't making a big to-do about Chuck Norris during 1985 was Norris himself. Typical.

Alternately nestled in his five-bedroom ranch house in the Rolling Hills section of Palos Verdes, blasting around town in a machine with

TOPKICK license plates, living the life of the country squire on his big northern California spread, and out on the road making films, it was just another in a long line of good years for Norris. "Yes," he told *The New York Times,* "I really appreciate the acclaim. I've worked hard these last nine years to get critics to look at me in a different light. They're usually more concerned with things like *Passage to India* and they've hit me hard all these years, especially in the beginning. I'm really excited, to say the least."

Yep, he was so darn worked up that he even took a couple of months off before he started making his next film. Perhaps some of this time was spent lolling around in his hot tub sucking down Chuck Norris Kicker's (which he once described to the Los Angeles *Times* as "iced tea with a shot of Grand Marnier"), but it must be remembered that this is a man who begins every day (except Sunday) with a three-hour workout. Not just any workout, either. We're talking three hours of hell. Three hours with Norris's personal trainer, former world kick-boxing champion Howard Jackson. Three hours that would kill a normal human being. Of course, Norris may be onto something. At a trim 5-foot-10 and 167 pounds, he reports that his weight has been the same for over twenty years.

Certainly Norris's almost superhuman physical prowess is, at least, partly responsible for his popularity. For this reason alone he'd be foolhardy to let himself go even slightly to seed. But

Norris is a straight arrow of such awesome proportions that it's easy to imagine he'd be doing the same routine even if he were still working as an office grunt for Northrup Aircraft.

After all, here's a man who has wrestled in the mud with the delectable Barbara Carrera, yet has repeatedly told the press that the biggest thrill in his life is that his sons "aren't embarrassed to kiss [him] hello and goodbye in front of everybody." Is he putting us on? It doesn't seem likely. And he does most of his own stunts, too—that was no stand-in risking life and limb with Carrera!

By all reports Chuck Norris, one of the toughest son of a mom's yet to stalk the earth, is also one of the gentlest, most down-to-earth and family-oriented souls you'd ever care to meet. His two sons, his wife of twenty-seven years, his brother, his co-workers, and even his four dogs all attest to this. As Ben Fong-Torres wrote in *Moviegoer,* "Norris's capacity for steady hard work, matched with an almost legendary evenness of temper, elicits great loyalty and respect. Ask around and you find that his colleagues' opinions of him are about as diverse as their opinions of motherhood and the flag." This theme has run through much of the press Norris has generated over the years, and while visions of him as a relaxed, pleasant guy may be at odds with the roles he plays (and the image he projects), they really are not so far apart at all.

Consider Norris's on-screen characters. The most obvious thing about them is their ability to retaliate promptly and completely when provoked. Quite often they strike like vengeful angels sweeping down en masse from the heavens to mop up the sinners amongst us, and the resultant carnage usually does "clean the house." The crucial factor here, however, is that Norris's avengers don't fly off the handle. They don't explode until they're provoked—and they're usually provoked plenty. If anything, his heroes are a bit reluctant to trounce the bad guys until pushed far beyond the limits of an average person's self-control. This is certainly in keeping with Norris's personal style, and one would also hope it's second nature for anyone with even a fraction of his prowess in the martial arts field.

As Norris told writer James Truman, "The only person who has made me feel threatened since I began studying the martial arts is my wife. She can certainly out-talk me." She probably could not out-slug him, though, and there are precious few people who could. This knowledge must make it easier to walk through life with a genuine smile on your face. But it is knowledge that can only be gleaned via many years of intense study, and the philosophical outlook that is required for a true mastery of karate precludes aggression.

Norris put it this way to a reporter from the Houston *Post*: "Karate gives you confidence that whatever happens you can handle it. It's essentially a defensive measure. Let's say you're in a club with your wife and some loudmouth troublemaker comes in and starts making a scene. You're thinking, 'Oh gosh, I sure hope he doesn't come over here.' Well, I don't think that. That doesn't mean I could go over there and waste the guy—who knows, he might beat me—but karate has taught me not to worry about it. Ever. That's the thing most people don't understand about it —karate is a thing of the spirit." He explained it once as being "like the mild-mannered Clark Kent knowing he can turn into Superman, except I don't go into a phone booth and change into a karate uniform."

Norris is a great admirer of and believer in Teddy Roosevelt's "Speak softly and carry a big stick" philosophy. As he once complained to the New Orleans *Times Picayune*: "Everybody assumes martial artists are ferocious people. Whenever I'm on *The Johnny Carson Show* or *The Merv Griffin Show* they expect me to break things. And although I'm all for teaching karate in the public schools, most boards of education are against it. They say, 'We don't want our kids to be killers.' But in fact, karate experts are modest and very controlled. Karate is not a game or a sport—it's an art, which is why we refer to it as one of the martial arts."

Karate requires that its practitioners successfully unite their minds and bodies, and those without the purity of motive to do this will never succeed at any of the martial arts. That Norris has been extremely successful at several of them should go without saying.

Although people becoming acquainted with Norris through his recent movies may think of him the way he'd like to be thought of—as an action-adventure film star—long-time fans are more aware of his karate prowess, so abundantly displayed in earlier films. In movies like *A Force of One* and *The Octagon,* the central attraction was Norris's lightning-fast dispatch of the primary villains without ever resorting to weaponry. Probably due to budgetary limitations as much as anything else, the arsenals available to his characters in recent films were not evident earlier. And hell, he didn't need any weapons anyway.

Norris was well-known and respected in martial arts circles long before his face was plastered fifty feet high on the silver screen. He was the undefeated world professional middleweight karate champ for six years running, and Bruce Lee's sparring partner for two-and-a-half years. He is the author of best-selling instructional books and was one of the earliest occidental exponents of "The Art of the Empty Hand."

His high profile as a tournament fighter and teacher served as Norris's entry to films. Without it he would probably be a member of the Torrance Police Department (his original plan) rather than "The Toughest Cop in the World" (as he was billed for *Code of Silence*). You can only wonder which of these professions makes the world a safer place.

As he told James Truman, "Training in martial arts develops you in many areas—physically, mentally, psychologically, emotionally. Through discipline, martial arts creates a better self-image." This is something that's very important to Norris and it's something that he's spent much of his movie career trying to instill in his viewers by playing only roles that present a positive image (especially to his younger, more impressionable fans). In the press kit for *Missing in Action 2: The Beginning,* he is quoted as saying, "I'll never play a drug addict or an alcoholic. When I do films, whatever role I play, in the kids' eyes, it's Chuck Norris up there on screen, not the guy I'm portraying." He adds, "I just wouldn't do anything on screen that would be detrimental to that image and possibly damaging to the kids. As long as I figure as a role model, I want to be a positive one. I hope to project an image kids can relate to and emulate."

He also remarked to a writer from the Los Angeles *Times* that none of his characters would ever hit a woman. "To me, that makes you less than a man. You will never see me playing a character that I think could be harmful for kids. There are good guys and bad guys in my movies. What I really make is just a new kind of Western. The kids know that and so do their parents. They know my films are okay because I don't get into heavy-duty sex scenes. As far as I'm concerned, it's sex scenes that can harm a kid. That's a tension thing; sexual tension is something they can't release. But when they watch a fight scene, and start yelling and getting into the action, that's tension they can release."

In the press kit for *Invasion USA,* Norris describes his films as "a modern-day version of the old cowboy movies I grew up watching. In my movies the good guy always wins. There's somebody for the audience to cheer, somebody for them to identify with. In real life and in the roles I play on film I do not exploit my ability to fight. There is a difference between action and violence. I try to keep my fighting scenes artistic.

"The characters I portray use their skills only as a last resort. That's what I want people to take home from the theater. There has always been violence on the screen. Today they're trying to get into this doggone bit about what makes a criminal. They say, 'Well, this movie made him do it.' That's hogwash. We all have the potential to be violent. We have to learn to control it."

Far from abdicating responsibility for his characters' actions, he told *USA Today* that he has to be especially careful of his on-screen activities. "Whatever I do is gospel with my students. If I smoke dope or snort cocaine they might say, 'Well shoot, Chuck does it.' Discipline is missing in a lot of kids' lives today. It's missing in schools and at home . . . Kids will never say, 'Discipline me. I need it.' But they do." And one guy who has discipline to spare is Norris.

When Norris was in Chicago to film *Code of Silence,* the rotund film critic Roger Ebert dropped by the star's hotel room for an early morning interview and was treated to an abridged version of his exercise ritual. First, the furniture was pushed up against the walls. Then there was a half hour of stretching, followed by an hour of kicking, twenty minutes of punching, twenty minutes of sit-ups, twenty minutes of twisting a heavy spring, and twenty minutes of stretching a plastic skin-diving hose. Is that all? Yeah, this morning's constitutional was cut short because, Norris reasoned, "When we're in a hotel we don't do the jumping stunts because you tend to get complaints from the people in the room underneath yours."

Naturally, this regimen preceded a regular twelve-hour shooting schedule of the sort that's draining enough to keep most Hollywood types pasted to barstools when they're not on camera. As Norris has noted on numerous occasions, however, he is not a "Hollywood type." Furthermore, as he told the *Times Picayune,* "I can't see myself ever getting out of shape. I'm in my forties now and I'm as energetic as I was in my twenties. There's no age limit on karate, but you can quickly lose the necessary flexibility and agility if you skip training for even a few days." It's difficult to imagine him ever slacking off on his regimen, even if he did once gripe while shooting a movie that it was hard for him to get more exercise than he got in the fight scenes.

Norris is no shirker. He never has been, even when things were tough. As he told Truman, "Acting has been a real grind for me. So was karate, but I was young then. I was twenty-one. Fifteen years later when I decided to become an actor I was thirty-six. It's always tough. Because I know everything is hard for me, I accept it. I'm prepared to face the difficulty of it. I know it's not going to be handed to me. If I'm going to make it, it will be through a lot of hard work and effort."

But then, Norris has always maintained that the real message of his movies (yes, there is one) is to work hard and "be the best that you can be regardless of what it is that you pursue. That's what the characters I play do: they strive for the best." And if there was ever a case of typecasting, well, that's it. Looking back on Norris's achievements, you won't ever find him giving one iota less than his very best.

2

One cold and fateful night in Ryan, Oklahoma, 1939, the appearance of Carlos Ray Norris increased the world's population by one. His mother was a devout Baptist of Irish-English descent, his father a full-blooded Cherokee with an eye for the open road. Norris didn't pull any punches when he described his dad for *People* magazine. "He was a cliché: a drunken Indian." His mom, however, did double duty in order to balance out the errant father's shortcomings. She worked her fingers to the quick, taking in the neighbors' laundry and providing a good home for our man and his two younger brothers, Wieland and Aaron. Norris once described her as "very religious and very strict with us. We were extremely poor and often hungry, but there was always lots of love at home and from it we developed ideals and faith." Still, he recalls, "Our main concern was getting enough to eat."

Growing up in the Bible Belt that girds the Dust Bowl, while the Great Depression was a fresh wound on the face of the nation, was nothing but hard. To a child, however, even this new, harsh, less innocent world was bright and exciting. The realities of the economic destruction which still cast a pall over the area were felt by young Norris as a growling stomach and a lack of toys. The fact that his store of physical treasures was wanting, however, forced him to stretch his imagination in order to create new playthings out of the precious few items at hand. Oddly enough, he now feels that some of the boyhood romping he did with the household objects he found laying around may have foreshadowed events of his later life.

During the course of a lengthy interview with James Truman, Norris explained: "When I was a kid we didn't have money to buy toys or anything to play with, so I used clothespins. All the different sizes. I would always be the small one. I saw myself, even then, as the little guy going against the big guys. So I'd assemble armies and I'd be leading them against these big clothespins. The amazing thing was that when they were doing battle I'd have these clothespins get up and do kicks. Which was, of course, karate, although as a five-year-old kid I didn't know that. I couldn't have seen it on TV; there wasn't any television then. This was 1945. I went to the movies, but the movies didn't use karate in them. Now I'm grown up and I'm doing the same thing I was doing at five with clothespins. I don't know what the terminology is for making something you want materialize, but I think it can be done. It has in my life."

This power to make things happen at will is apparently not something Norris had mastered during his "Oklahoma Years." Otherwise he would have surely dealt a rather more vigorous and dreadful blow to the third-grade class bully than the one he described to a reporter from *USA Today*. As Norris recalled, there was a humongous Indian kid in his class who was the meanest little mountain the playground had ever seen. Cut from a classic bully-boy bolt, he pulled all sorts of mean Little Rascals-styled stunts on his fellow students. For reasons unknown, he bore a special animosity toward Chuck Norris and would chase him, screaming, from school to his front door every day. The young Norris was reportedly deft enough to elude the beast, but one day Norris Sr. (undoubtedly tired of the sight and sound of this daily grudge match) told his son, "That's enough. You've got to fight him." Norris the Younger slept on this and, still unsure of what he'd do, faced off against his tormenter the very next afternoon. As he puts it, "This kid was so big I just grabbed his finger and held on for dear life . . . He finally started crying and quit." Imagine the tears of shame streaming down the bully's face. If he'd known what was in store for that little kid riding his pinky he might not have been quite so embarrassed.

Even with this early victory neatly marked on his fight record, Norris didn't really have dreams of glory through fisticuffs. He's said that when he was six or seven he had absolutely no idea of what he wanted to be. Just getting by was enough for him. His mom had so much trouble making ends meet that his vision of the future didn't go too far past the next meal. His dad was so often absent from home that he provided little substance as a role model. In a few interviews, Norris has gone so far as to say that John Wayne was a "substitute father" to him, since he saw more of Wayne, on screen during Saturday matinees, than he did of his dad, in the flesh on Saturday or any other day. In his father's defense, it should be remembered that these were hard times, especially in this part of America and even more so for a displaced Native American.

While his dad floated across the parched landscape, Chuck became absorbed with the shadows that floated across the silver screen at the local movie house. The years immediately preceding and during the Second World War were responsible for producing some of the most heroic images ever to be imprinted on the American consciousness, and it was to these icons that Norris was drawn. His favorites, as he told Truman, were "John Wayne and Gary Cooper—the strong silent types. The Westerner was the man's man. A man who faced the odds, whether against a person, against the elements, whatever, and came out victorious. All my life I grew up idolizing people like that." How this relates to his own Indian heritage we can only speculate, but one aspect of the archetypal Westerner that must have appealed to Norris was his unwillingness to rely on any other man. He was, in short, a loner —and it was the loner's cloth from which Norris too was cut.

It's not that he didn't try to socialize, but the cards were surely stacked against his being the most popular boy in school. He was a half-breed, from a broken home, in the hinterlands of Oklahoma, and conspicuously poor even for the piss-poor town in which he lived. He claims to have been physically clumsy and, judging by the speaking voice in his early films, he must have had a bad lisp during his childhood. These are not the characteristics that make up a golden boy, and Norris had little choice but to be a loner.

Shortly after his father disappeared for the last time, Chuck and the remainder of his family packed up and made the classic Okie trek to the gold-paved streets of California. The 1950s had begun with a boom in the greater Los Angeles area and the South Bay tract house sprawl that looks so depressing today must have seemed like heaven in comparison to the dried husk of Ryan, Oklahoma. It was still a far cry from the pearly gates, though.

Even with the local aeronautics boom during those optimistic post-war years, the life of a single mother was nothing to sing about. The good jobs, which so many women had held during the years of conflict with the Axis, were neatly wrested from their hands when the boys came back home, and it was all Mrs. Norris could do to find drudge work at Northrup Aircraft.

The first blush of the Norris family's life in California was explained thusly to Truman: "My mother still took in laundry to support us. She worked in the aircraft factory from three till midnight. I came home from school and looked after my brother. My mother is a very strong force. She's a very religious person, and through her faith I got a lot of strength in my life. We were poor, but I wasn't unhappy in my life. Happiness isn't money or success or being a movie star. Look at half these actors—they're spaced out half the time on drugs. It's because they're not satisfied with their lives."

Norris was satisfied, even if school wasn't a whole lot of fun. He described himself to *People* magazine as "the shy kid who never excelled at anything in school." He still dreaded getting up in front of the class to deliver a book report, but no longer went to the extreme of playing ill on the day reports were due, as he'd done in Ryan. He went out for football and actually made the team at North Torrance High, but all he ever did was dust the bench with his behind. To Truman he described himself during this time as a bookworm: "I was pretty studious, very quiet, very reserved. I was not a quick learner, and school was tough for me." Luckily for this slowpoke, his whole system was about to get the jolt it needed.

One afternoon while he was a junior he crossed the path of a pretty, blonde sophomore named Dianne Holechek. Norris was apparently brooding over something and barely noticed her, but Dianne saw sparks. She grabbed her girl friend by the arm and solemnly pledged, "That's the guy I'm going to marry." Norris is fond of recalling that he was so painfully shy it took him three months to ask Dianne out for a date, even though she repeatedly sent emissaries to assure him that she was indeed waiting for him to do so. In the Fifties it was unimaginable that a girl would ask a boy for a date, so wait Dianne did, and her patience must have been wearing kind of thin by the time Norris finally worked up the nerve.

Once he jumped, though, let it not be said that Norris was a hesitant suitor. The Los Angeles *Times* reports that it was not far into their romance that Chuck took Dianne for a date on the Long Beach Pike (a carny sort of strip that was quite a seedy spot for its time) and, in a frenzy of JD-style troth-pledging, had her Christian name attached to his left forearm (permanent-like) in a tattoo parlor. As he has since noted, "It's a damn good thing I married her. You don't find too many Diannes who spell their name with two n's." Quite true.

So, to spare him any such embarrassment, Dianne married her ink-embossed Romeo shortly after he graduated from North Torrance High School and enlisted in the Air Force. He signed up because he'd decided during his last spell of schooling that he wanted to be a cop. He didn't really think he was cut out for college, and in those days you either went to college or put in your years in the service. The United States was not at war with anyone then, so that was no great danger and, furthermore, he figured he might be able to pick up some education in the Air Force which would help him achieve his goal of becoming a policeman after his hitch had been served. To this end he actually did take some courses in criminology and police science and even became an MP.

Stationed in Osan, Korea, Norris soon had his first true exposure to the martial arts. Although there are reports of English and American athletes studying the rudiments of judo and some of the other Japanese martial arts as early as 1900, knowledge of this sort was extremely rare until the Second World War ended and the soldiers stationed in Japan returned home with tales of the Orient's so-called "soft arts." These mysterious techniques reportedly enabled even small men to grapple with giants through leverage, sharply focused power, and intense concentration.

Interestingly, one of the primary public arenas for display of these arts was the professional wrestling ring. In the early days of television, pro wrestling was a staple in almost every home that had a TV, and the moves of wrestlers like Wild Bill Koury and Johnny Valentine were frequently described by ringside commentators as being traceable back to the Asian continent. That this was usually a load of bologna made no difference. Many Americans were made familiar with at least some martial arts terminology through the magic of wrestling, and Norris may have well been among their number. At any rate, he decided to pursue the art most often spoken of in the United States: judo.

Judo (an official Olympic sport since the 1964 Summer Games in Tokyo) is known as a "soft art" because it is primarily a defensive system. The practitioner does not oppose his attacker's force, but uses the incoming force against itself to defeat the attacker. The idea is to evade the attacker's thrust and to then subdue him with holds and locks. It is not oriented toward aggressive movement at all and the introverted Norris took to it like Tom Trot's dog.

Not that his motives were as pure as all that. As he told the New Orleans *Times Picayune,* he decided to take up not just to help round him for a law enforcement career, but also because "there wasn't much to do there and I wanted to be a mean guy. I didn't realize then that aggressiveness comes from shyness and insecurity."

Studying judo on the base at Osan, Norris began to have new insights into himself, but his training was not without its setbacks. The would-be policeman had not been involved with judo for long when he broke his shoulder during a particularly dicey workout. With his arm in a sling for an indefinite period, extensive daily judo practice was impractical (not to mention painful), so he began to spend his free afternoons wandering through the hamlets that surrounded the base. "One day," he told Truman, "I was just out walking in a village and I saw these Koreans working out in a field, throwing these spectacular kicks. I was mesmerized, and watching those guys I thought, 'Jeez, I can't believe what they're doing.'"

Norris watched the men for a long while, then rushed back to the base and described what he had seen to his judo instructor. He demanded to know what it was that they were doing and his sensei replied that it was Tang Soo Do, a Korean version of karate. As Norris recalls, "I'd never even heard the word *karate* before. Nobody had. Judo was the big thing, but my sensei explained what it was to me and introduced me to another sensei who taught Tang Soo Do."

Norris was so eager to begin that he commenced training while his arm was still in a sling. After the arm healed, he began to study karate more diligently. Unlike judo, karate is one of the "hard arts." In fighting systems of this style, force is opposed by force. Arms and legs are directed to strike with great intensity in straight lines from the body. There is still much blocking and parrying, but karate is designed to be offensive as well as defensive. It gives one what might be called "first strike capability." By all reports, Norris was even more naturally adept at this than he had been at judo.

After his arm had properly healed, however, Norris did return to studying judo. He described his practice schedule as follows: "I trained in karate Monday through Saturday from five to ten at night, then in judo on Sunday for five hours. These studies changed my entire outlook on life. For the first time I realized that there was nothing I couldn't achieve if I just had determination and persistence. In gaining the ability to defend myself, I also learned the discipline and self-respect I needed for the rest of my life."

By the time he left Korea, Norris had earned a brown belt in judo and a black belt in Tang Soo Do as testament to his prowess. He returned to the States in 1961. At this time he still had a year to go in his enlistment and was stationed in Riverside, California. He continued to function as an MP, which gave him an opportunity to use some of the "controlling-type techniques" he'd learned. No doubt he was plenty effective as a peacekeeper. He also taught karate to fellow servicemen during this Stateside tour of duty. Invited to address an assembly of four hundred persons, convened by the base's karate club, he called upon the new wells of discipline that had been tapped by his training.

He described it this way to an Associated Press wire reporter: "This was the first time that I ever had to get up in front of a large crowd and give a talk. I was twenty-one years old and I had never made a speech before. I had two weeks to memorize the short speech I'd written and I'd been rehearsing and practicing it so much that I'd overprepared. When I faced the audience of four hundred, my hands were sweating and I nearly forgot everything I had intended to say. I recited that speech as if I were in a trance and afterwards I wondered, 'Did I say anything?' That experience was enough to crack the edge of my insecurity. I am sure it was the physical ability I'd developed in the martial arts that gave me the self-confidence to do something I'd never done before, and after that I had no trouble facing audiences."

Not too long after his public-speaking debut, in 1962, Norris received his honorable discharge from the Air Force. He was now free to achieve his goal and become a member of the Torrance police force. He took the exam immediately. The civil service did its standard snail-paced digestion of his test results and application, and Norris waited for quite a while to hear back from them. The bills couldn't just be put on "hold" and Dianne was expecting her first baby, so Norris took a job working for his mom's old employer—Northrup Aircraft. He's since said, "It was the first job I was offered and I had to take it."

His position as a file clerk paid the princely sum of $325 per month and, especially after his first son, Mike, was born, this wasn't quite enough to make ends meet. In order to add some more money to the pot he decided to make the most of his martial talents and opened a karate school near his home. He was still planning to go to the police academy eventually, but his first responsibility was to keep his family maintained. He would work at Northrup from eight to five, drive by the house, where Dianne would hand him a sandwich, and then go right to the school, wearing one of the karate uniforms she'd sewn for him.

He continued to toil in this fashion for two years, either working, teaching, or training virtually every hour of the day. Then, right about the time his second son, Eric, was born, he came to the realization that he'd probably never end up a cop. His karate school was thriving, he was on the point of opening other branches, and so in 1964 he quit Northrup and began teaching full-time. It was a decision he would never regret.

3

In 1964, when Norris decided to devote all his attention to karate, the martial arts were still considered rank chicanery by most of the American populace. The taste of Stateside fight fans had "matured" to the point where they no longer yearned for the scientific wrestling techniques of Professor Toru Tanaka (a Tai Chi Chu'an master). They were more intrigued by the less graceful slugging of hulking palookas like Sonny Liston. Karate was one of the first martial arts to gain any popularity in America. Yet, as *Spin* magazine noted, "In 1964, karate wasn't much heard of outside a small network of enthusiasts and a few lurid come-on's of the 'Render Assailants Powerless in Ten Seconds' type, tucked away next to the toupee ads in the back pages of *Boxing Illustrated.*"

How true. Happily, Norris was based in California, where many of the few karate enthusiasts were located. By running a school, as he did, he became the hub around which local activity spun. In these pioneer days of martial arts in

America, the few extant karate schools were more than mere academies. They were central meeting halls where the rare folk who pursued this esoteric art could meet to swap stories and tips and blows. This was especially true of Norris's schools, since he was not only a teacher but a stylistic innovator as well.

In the preface to *Winning Tournament Karate* (Ohara Publications, Burbank, CA 1975), John Robertson calls Norris "the initiator of a truly Americanized karate." He notes that Norris first dedicated years to learning the essence of Korea's Tang Soo Do and then departed from the rigorous stylistic strictures of the form's classical interpretation. Tang Soo Do (like Tae Kwon Do and Hwarang Do, the other primary fighting systems born in Korea) is heavily reliant on powerful high kicks, which are often performed while the practitioners are airborne. Its hand usage is somewhat less distinctive, owing debts to the "hard arts" schools of both Japan and Mainland China. This is not too odd, considering that Korea is a peninsula that sits midway between these two seats of martial-art theory. So, in a sense, Tang Soo Do is already an integrative art. But if this integration was mostly limited to minor hand movements borrowed from China's Shaolin tradition and, perhaps, Japan's Shorinji Kempo, Norris's version of it added more colorfully international threads.

Where traditionalists relied primarily on their legs as weapons of choice, Norris placed an equal emphasis on the hands and arms. His approach incorporated techniques drawn from numerous Oriental styles as well as English-style boxing (perhaps the only purely indigenous Western form of unarmed combat) and some of the methodology practiced by his friend Bruce Lee, the father of Jeet Kune Do (or "The Way of the Exploding Fist").

By the time Norris had finished crossing all these seemingly irreconcilable strains of the martial-arts virus, he had developed a unique hybrid. And while he continued to identify it as Tang Soo Do, it became popularly known as the Chuck Norris Blitz. Easily identified, it manifested itself as what *Spin* called "a fearsome whirlwind attack of hands and feet topped off with a signature spin-back sidekick." With it Norris was virtually unstoppable. Where the training of most martial artists forced them to rely on either their feet or hands, Norris had made himself a truly all-around fighter: it was like two fighting men in one. And where better to use these extra limbs than in a competitive situation?

Norris decided to become a tournament karate fighter soon after he became a karate professional. He reasoned that entering the world of tournament competition could only help solidify his position in the martial-arts community. He had black belts in both Tang Soo Do and Tae Kwan Do and was beginning to be acknowledged as the master of his own school of fighting. Not a man of false modesty, he felt that he could be a world-class competitor once he hit his stride.

There could be no better advertising for his schools than that.

Another factor that made karate competition so appealing to Norris was his own desire to keep his skills honed and ready. Since he'd returned from Korea he'd often felt he was backsliding a bit in his sparring, due to the lack of available expert opponents. He figured he'd meet some truly worthy opposition if he'd make the effort to search it out. So he did.

The first tournament Norris entered was held in Salt Lake City, some 750 miles from his home base in Torrance. Norris encouraged three of his students to sign up as well. Together, they drove for sixteen straight hours to reach the meet. Tired and cramped from the overlong confinement in Norris's Ford Falcon, the quartet was not in optimum shape to compete, but that didn't stop them. Each fought in turn and three of them came away winners. Strangely, the only one to lose his bout was Norris. Chuck meditated on the whys and wherefores of this loss all through the long drive back through the barren Southwest desert. At first he just brooded over the mistakes he'd made, but he eventually realized that the real reason he'd lost was that he hadn't adequately learned from past experiences and failures.

As he explained in *Toughen Up* (Bantam Books, New York City, 1983): "I realized that failure can be the key to success if you are willing to learn. Because I could learn from the experience of that first tournament, I hadn't really lost at all." When he was back in training at home he replayed the fight in his mind and tried out alternative strategies. Soon, he was able to overcome the sequences of moves that had beaten him in his tournament debut. At this point he felt ready to venture out again. While he was defeated again, it was not by any method that had previously bested him. Once more he woodshedded and ran through the fight again and again. In his next competition (the 1965 Winter Nationals in San Jose), he scored his first big win and captured the California State Title. "That's when I knew I'd learned a really important lesson about life," Norris wrote. "You can improve yourself through the mistakes you make."

This is an excellent example of the kind of philosophy on which the martial arts (especially the "soft" ones) are built. Much Eastern philosophy contains a concept similar to the Chinese *yin* and *yang*—the basic oppositional elements of dark and light from which everything is made. The Japanese call these same elements *in* and *yo* and they are something like two poles of a magnet constantly moving toward each other. In the Eastern style of thought, every object contains the seed of its own opposite and is continually in the state of changing into it. And as it's impossible to become a master of karate (or any other martial art) without having a firm grasp of Eastern philosophy, it's not surprising that Norris was able to convert his losses into victories with not too much effort. This was merely one more step along the path of spiritual development that parallels the technical development of any true practitioner of "the art of the empty hand." An original thinker even in this area, Norris cooked up an ethical code of his own to pass on to his students.

He told Truman, "I've blended the Eastern and Western philosophies together. That's what I've done. I think you must have an ego in order to strive. Like, when I was a fighter someone would ask, 'Can you beat this guy?' I'd say, 'Jeez, I don't know. It's going to take a lot of luck for me to win.' I'm saying that, but all the time in my mind I'm thinking, 'Hey! I'm going to beat that sucker.' The thing is to control that ego. I've read a lot of books by people like Norman Vincent Peale [author of *The Power of Positive Thinking*] and applied a lot of their philosophies to my life, along with Eastern philosophies, too. Your mind is able to conceive of what is not in the realm of possibility, and karate better enables you to achieve your goals. I think that's what really worked for me—the blend of the two.

"In my schools we have all this philosophy in our constitution that students have to learn. Very poppy-like things that students have to repeat in class. Like, 'If you don't have nothing good to say about somebody, just don't say anything.' Things like that. Because when people come in and say they want to learn karate, you have to analyze what they're saying. If they say they want to know how to kick or punch or chop, that's not really the reason. What they're saying is, 'Make me feel stronger as a person. Make me have that better security in myself and have a better self-image.' The physical thing is just the method, and there aren't many methods that give as much. Karate—the martial arts—is probably the only method that can strengthen you in so many areas. That's the greatest thing the martial arts have. Unfortunately, a lot of schools don't do that."

And karate schools were beginning to pop up like weeds, even as Norris was starting to make a name for himself on the martial arts scene. Using his unique Blitz techniques, Norris cut through the competition like an enormous scythe. "If you want to win, play to win," he has often been quoted as saying, and that's just what he did. Having taken the 1965 California title in San Jose, he successfully defended it later that year. This accomplished, he continued his ascent through the different levels of competition in the middleweight division (164 to 172 pounds) with the clenched-jawed tenacity for which he's known. He later remarked to *The New York Times*: "When I started I never thought that I would be the world karate champion. All I wanted to do was win the California title, but after I'd won that, my goals increased."

Norris kept pace with these goals too. In 1967 he swept the All-American New York Grand Championships (a feat he repeated in 1968), then went on to do the same at the International Grand Championships in Long Beach, California. The best was still to come, though—and it arrived at Madison Square Garden in 1968 when

Norris became the Professional Middleweight Karate Champion of the World. He defended this title successfully until he retired from tournament fighting in 1974. If what he really wanted from competition was to make his name known in the field and keep his skills at a high level of excellence, it's tough to see how he could have done it better.

He was typically restrained when recounting his tournament career for Truman. "When I look back on winning the ultimate title," he said. "I realize that the most exciting moments are winning the local tournaments and the smaller titles. You look back and think, 'Those were the most enjoyable and exciting moments of this whole escapade.'"

Of course Norris didn't stop after winning the World Belt. Describing the six years following the World Class win, he said, "All I did was teach and fight." He makes it sound easy and relaxed, but the very next year (1969) he managed to win the National Tournament of Champions in Washington D.C., being awarded the Triple Crown for the highest number of tournament wins, and when *Black Belt* magazine decided to name a "Fighter of the Year," he was the hands-down favorite.

Norris's rise through the ranks of karate fighters was paralleled by the rise of karate's popularity in the United States. Veterans returning from Japan had begun the flow of knowledge about martial arts; those coming back from Korea had added to the pool of information; and the men returning from Vietnam-era tours of duty in the Orient added new insights about the once unknown "hard arts." The philosophical aspects of martial arts, once deemed peculiar and suspect by earlier groups of doughboys, actually added to its appeal with the soldiers coming of age in the Sixties and they took to it with unprecedented zeal.

The public at large now had at least a cursory notion of the martial arts. In the movies, the success of James Bond's Japanese arch-nemesis, Odd Job, spawned an army of chopping, kicking, grunting imitators. On television, ABC's Green Hornet series featured Bruce Lee as the Hornet's combination chauffeur/back-up squadron, and kids all over the country pantomimed Lee's balletic hijinks. Even in ads, you could see the Wildroot Man dispatching villains with one neat slice of the hand, and one company had the gall to market an aftershave called Hai Karate (which would presumably allow the wearer to smell like a martial-arts champ even if he was just an office boy).

In this environment, newly receptive to thousand-year-old ideas, Norris flourished. Besides festooning his belt with scalp after scalp, he appeared on numerous TV talk shows to be interviewed by the likes of Johnny Carson, Flip Wilson, Mike Douglas, and Merv Griffin; expanded his string of schools until there were seven operating in the Greater Los Angeles area; and trained a team of competitors who went undefeated for twenty-nine straight tournaments.

The schools were especially important to Norris, since unlike some fly-by-night operations (whose rip-off contracts Norris's academies would often honor "in order to keep up the industry's overall reputation"), their aim was to help sharpen every aspect of their students' lives. Especially the younger students.

"It's hard for kids today," Norris remarked to Truman. "They have so much to begin with, compared to kids in any other country. Sometimes that's good, sometimes that's bad. If you have everything to start with, you don't have that drive to succeed. I mean, I live in a very affluent area and those rich kids are just as miserable as any kid who's extremely poor in the ghetto. The whole thing, whether rich or poor, is knowing what to do with your life and then working towards that. That's excitement: the thrill of accomplishing, or overcoming obstacles that are in the way of whatever it is you're trying to achieve. It's exciting when there's an obstacle to hurdle and you work, work, work until you finally overcome that obstacle. You say, 'Wow, that was tough.' But at the same time it builds an inner strength in you to push even harder.

"That's what kids have to realize today to avoid the drug scene. Drugs are an artificial high. You go up and you have to come down. I believe that if our country is going to go down the tubes it will be because of drugs. They're the single worst thing in our country today. But if you're working towards a goal, and you're getting closer to achieving it and you're excited about it, then it's a constant high. That's the whole basis of life itself. You need that excitement.

"Like Elvis," Norris continued. "You saw what happened to him. He ran out of goals. He just didn't know what to do with himself. If he had just set himself a new goal, like working with underprivileged children, something that would have given him some gratification, then his life wouldn't have been so miserable." Norris didn't believe this angst was limited to superstars of Elvis's calibre, though. As Norris told the *Houston Post,* "I see kids coming into the schools who are obviously failure-oriented. They have negative esteem, poor attitude, whatever you want to call it. I see what karate has done for them, how they begin to develop a sense of their own worth when they see what they can accomplish. We start them as early as five years old and we even have them bring in their report cards. We're interested in the total person, not just how many bricks they can break."

Some students were interested only in the physical aspect of karate, though, and they were warned off by Norris when he discovered their intent. "You don't learn karate in two or three months," he declared. "It takes two or three years minimum. And that's three to four classes a week. We get these hotshots coming in who want to study for six weeks, then go out and terrorize the world. When they learn they're going to spend the first year just learning to block punches, they say, 'Hmmm. Well, maybe I'll just use a tire tool instead.' "

A jack handle will not really serve as a stand-in for a year's karate training, however, and business at Norris's schools was brisk. But after a few years, even though he was the reigning tournament champ and a powerful tutorial force, Norris began to get restless.

A man of action, he began to hatch a plan to fight this ennui. He refused to get caught up in a spiral of brooding, boredom, and worry. "My wife's a worrier," he told Truman. "And I've never been able to understand the process. I ask her, 'What good is worrying about something?' The thing is, when you worry it clogs up your creative senses and you can't work your way out of it. If you don't work your way out of it, the worry's not going to do you any good anyway. If you do work your way out of it, the worry was for nought. The best thing to do is not to worry about it and just get the job done the best way you can. That's a philosophy I've created that I live by. Sometimes I fall out of it. I'll start getting into some kind of depressed state, maybe even a little bit of hostile emotion and so I have to regroup and say, 'Hey—get your act together.' "

Taking his own advice literally, Norris decided to turn his gaze away from South Bay martial-arts circles. His eyes lit on a town a few miles to the north. A town where "getting your act together" has a very special meaning. A town called Hollywood.

4

Norris's first brush with the medium of film came soon after he'd won his first World Championship in 1968. Dean Martin was starring, as Matt Helm, in a series of spoofs on the 007-style action pictures that were so popular around the time. Based on books by Don Hamilton, four of these films were made in all. In the last of them, *Wrecking Crew,* there were several roles for karate experts and one such place was filled by Norris's willing body. It was only a bit part and had no bearing on the actual plot, but it is significant as Norris's screen debut. Norris wasn't really looking for film credentials at this point, but the movie industry was close at hand, and a few extra bucks never hurt. Unlike, say, boxing, where multi-million-dollar purses are common for bouts between top-seeded rivals, tournament karate is budgeted at a much lower level. Prizes are usually counted in hundreds of dollars rather than hundreds of thousands, and even the winningest fighters are not averse to a little moonlighting.

Norris's next couple of appearances on screen also fall under the category of moonlighting. The first of these was in a movie called *Student Teachers,* which he did in 1970. The film, Norris was told, was about a karate teacher who wavers, then breaks away, from conventional teaching methods. This sounded pretty jake to Norris and he didn't hesitate to film his scene. It showed him teaching a group of his actual pupils (including his sons Mike and Eric) and was shot in one afternoon, after which he promptly forgot about it. Several months later he was in San Francisco with his family and read in the newspaper that *Student Teachers* was opening locally during their stay. "I turned to Dianne and said, 'Let's go see that,' " he told James Truman. Reasoning that it would be a special treat for Mike and Eric to see themselves in Cinemascope, they decided to make a family outing of it.

And so the Norris clan set off for *Student Teachers'* gala debut. The film was playing in San Francisco's Tenderloin district (an area of inexpensive residence hotels and "adult" entertainments) and Norris remembers being surprised to find himself in the seediest part of town. "We get into the theater," he told Truman, "and people are smoking pot and all this . . . you know, there're a lot of perverts in there. So we sit down, the movie opens, and the first image on the screen is this naked woman getting out of bed and parading around the room. So we're desperately hiding Mike and Eric's eyes [the boys were then five and seven, respectively] with our hands.

Dianne wants to leave, but I say, 'Let's wait for our part. It can't be too long.' Well our part finally arrives, but only after about nineteen million sex scenes—this movie was the very next thing to an X. I was so embarrassed I didn't want to do any more kung-fu movies."

Well, Norris couldn't have been too embarrassed, because the very next year (1971) he got involved in another low-budget film, shot under the title *Yellow Faced Tiger.* He reported it this way to Truman: "I got this call from a Chinese film production company. They were in San Francisco shooting this film and they were looking for karate guys. I go up and they tell me I'm going to be this mafia boss. I say, 'Yeah, sure.' So they buy me a cheap suit and give me this stogie that's about two feet long. And I don't even smoke! I never saw the movie, but I should only be in it about ten minutes. During that time I try to rape my brother's girl friend and then at the end, this Chinese guy beats the living daylights out of me. At the time I couldn't have cared less, even though I hate to lose at anything. I didn't like the idea of losing, even in a movie, but when I went up for it I had no idea what I was going to do. Of course, once my movies became popular they brought it back from China, renamed it *Slaughter in San Francisco,* and claimed I was the star. I'm only in it for those ten minutes though."

These were not auspicious dealings with the film world by any stretch of the imagination. Soured by his brushes with penny-ante pornographers, Norris might well have avoided further dealings with the industry if he hadn't gotten a call early in 1973 from an old friend named Bruce Lee. Norris and Lee had first met in New York City at a tournament in the mid-Sixties. Both had fighting styles that encompassed a far wider assortment of techniques than those employed by most of their peers and they became quick pals. They also became sparring partners when Lee, after receiving a degree in philosophy from the University of Washington, decided to try his hand at acting and moved to Southern California.

In Los Angeles, Lee landed the role of Kato, an all-purpose sidekick to the Green Hornet. The Green Hornet was a crimefighting character who'd been born in the golden days of radio. ABC had decided to revive the Hornet and contemporize him in an effort to duplicate the great success of the comic-book-hero-turned-TV-star, Batman. The effort was none too successful. *The Green Hornet* proved to be fairly popular with a certain segment of the audience, but the numbers weren't with it and it only ran from September 1966 through the following June.

During *The Green Hornet*'s run, Lee was based in L.A. and he and Norris regularly worked out together. When the series was cancelled, Lee had a few guest spots on the *Batman* series and an occasional walk-on karate-related spot in the movies. This was not what he was after, though, and he eventually returned to his native Hong Kong (after about two-and-a-half years in L.A.) to investigate some film offers he'd gotten from there.

The first two movies Lee starred in were *The Big Boss* and *Fists of Fury*. In these films he projected an incredible charisma and showcased an amazing technical ability. Both films raked in unprecedented amounts of lucre and are generally credited for creating the kung-fu film craze of the early Seventies. Contracted by producer Raymond Chow to do a third film, Lee announced that this one would have a climactic battle that would beggar description. Chuck says that Lee just called him one day and said he was making a film with a really terrific fight sequence. Would he be interested? For anyone else the answer might have been, "No." But Lee was a friend and Norris thought it might be fun. It was.

The movie was called *Return of the Dragon* and it represents the high water mark achieved by kung-fu filmmakers, not least because of the amazing battle between Norris and Lee. Briefly, the film tells the story of a Chinese restaurant in Rome and the trouble that befalls its owners when they won't play along with local heavies. Lee, playing a country bumpkin-cum-master-fighter named Tang Lung, gets called in from the old country and takes care of the competition without raising a sweat. Obviously, big guns are called for to dispose of this pesky bumpkin and "money is no object." Consequently, the mobsters send a fat wad of green to the States to rent the services of America's best—a guy known only as "Colt." Guess who? Bingo.

After trashing the masters from Japan and Europe, Colt proceeds to the Roman Colosseum for an appointment with Tang Lung, and their fight is legend among fans of celluloid mayhem. Precisely choreographed and executed, the two strike and parry with a rare grace. And even though Norris has to lose (it is, after all, Bruce's film), he goes down about as easily as an adrenaline-pumped rhino. Luckily for his career to come, Norris was also laid out in style, as befitting a warrior who was Lee's equal. This, in contrast to the quick send-offs provided most of Bruce's adversaries.

"It's fortunate," Norris told Truman, "that Bruce, being a friend, didn't make me out to be that bad a character. He built it up more like two gladiators pitting their skills against each other. When he killed me he put the uniform and belt over me very ceremoniously, so the audience didn't boo me. I had no desire just then to be an actor and I didn't know what the devil I was doing in the first place, but it was lucky for me that Bruce handled it that way. Otherwise I would have been typecast as a bad guy. So it really worked out well. It gave me a degree of international popularity.

"But there was a negative side to that, too, because when I started doing my own pictures they immediately put me in the Bruce Lee category as a kung-fu actor. If I hadn't done that movie and had jumped in and done a little bit of martial arts, like I did in *Breaker! Breaker!* and *Good Guys Wear Black,* they wouldn't have classified me as a "chop socky" actor, which is what I had to deal with." He didn't have to deal with it immediately though, since he returned to his schools and teaching as soon as the film was completed.

Back in the States, however, his mind kept returning to that fight under the lights at the Colosseum and the other scenes he'd been in prior to it. He was hooked on the idea of making movies. This feeling became even stronger when he learned how much money it was possible to make in the field. For instance, *Return of the Dragon,* reportedly costing a total of $135,000 to make, grossed over *sixty million dollars* in ticket sales.

Those kind of figures suggested possibilities to Norris. He was not interested in involving himself in projects that would compromise his personal integrity, however, so the first flurry of bids for his screen appearance were given the bum's rush.

Shortly after *Return of the Dragon* came out and began breaking box-office records, Bruce Lee died of a brain hemmorhage. His death, at the age of thirty-two, shocked fans all around the world, but no one reacted quite so sharply as the men who'd been producing his films. Their golden goose had been snatched from them and all he'd left behind was a six-minute fight scene with Kareem Abdul-Jabbar that was scheduled to be used in his next film, *The Game of Death.* Looking for a name-brand fighter to help them finish the picture, they quickly got in touch with

Chuck. Norris told them he thought it would be a ripoff for him to help them finish the film and then promote it as Bruce Lee's last. They used him anyway, taking parts of his fight scene with Lee from *Return of the Dragon* and splicing them in where needed. This may sound like dirty pool, but it was actually one of the least offensive exploitation moves pulled by the "chop socky" film industry in the wake of Lee's last gasp.

As the *Wall Street Journal* reported: "Bruce Lee's name lives on and on and on . . . Since the release of the actor's last feature film, the name Bruce Lee has turned up in at least forty kung-fu motion pictures, most of them shot in Hong Kong or Taiwan. Many of the Lee pictures have used the Lee name in the title—such films as *Young Bruce Lee, Bruce Lee Returns from the Dead,* and *The Return of Bruce.* A dozen other kung-fu epics have starred actors with such names as Bruce Lai, Bruce Li, Lee Bruce, Dragon Lee, and Myron Bruce Lee." Had he wished it, any number of these "epics" could have featured Norris.

"You know, right after Bruce Lee died, I got offers to do tons of similar kung-fu movies," he told the Houston *Post.* "But I turned them all down. It was all that meaningless violence, fight after fight. I don't mean to cut down Bruce, he was trying to make the transition, to instill his films with some of the philosophy behind martial arts when he died."

The standard "chop socky" fare never really appealed to Norris's aesthetic palate. Asked by

Truman if he was a fan of the genre, he replied, "I've only seen two of them. Basically, I feel they're too phony. A lot of the Hong Kong movies just have people flying through the air executing impossible maneuvers. Lee was different. Lee was real real good. He never fought professionally, but he was a good technician." And although Lee was a very good martial artist, according to Norris, he "was no mystic."

For this reason, as Norris told the New Orleans *Times Picayune,* he could never understand why "such a cult has grown up about him since his death. I lived across the street from Bruce's widow and he died of an aneurism—just plain natural causes. But lots of his fans are convinced to this day that there was some mystery to his death or that he will come back to life. And then there are all these ripoffs. They've used every last foot of film he ever shot and there are all those actors running around with names like Bruce Li. I hope that doesn't repeat itself if something happens to me. Can you imagine a half dozen actors running around named Charley Morris?"

"Still," Norris added while talking to the Houston *Post,* "in certain ways, Bruce's death might have done some good because there has been a downslide in the kung-fu craze. When it was hot there were about nineteen million schools opened up to cash in on it and ninety percent were no good. People were buying black belts, not earning them. There's no regulatory agency, no anything. You could rent a warehouse and open a school tomorrow. If you have a good gift of gab, you'd probably sell a lot of lessons. After Lee's death this trend lost some of its momentum. It's still going strong, but it did stabilize in the Seventies."

So did Norris. In 1974 he retired, undefeated, as World Professional Middleweight Champion and tried to decide what he should tackle next. A possibility soon suggested itself. "I was in Hong Kong doing *Return of the Dragon,*" he told Truman, "when I saw a movie called *On Any Sunday* that featured Steve McQueen. And I thought, 'God I'd like to meet that guy. I think we could be friends.' I come back from doing the movie with Bruce and about two months later I'm in my karate school and one of the guys says, 'Hey, it's Steve McQueen on the phone.' His son had just lost a fight and he wanted to see about having me teach him karate. So he brings Chad down and we meet. Then Steve started taking lessons and we became good friends."

Norris, it should be noted, had something of a reputation as a karate teacher to numerous Hollywood luminaries. His client list included such glittering stars as Bob Barker, Marie Osmond, Priscilla Presley, and many more. One interesting sidelight to his tutorial of Mrs. Presley is that Norris is the one responsible for introducing her to Mike Stone, the karate fighter for whom she dumped the King!

After Norris stopped competing he began to feel complacent and unchallenged. When he finally decided he might like to try acting he decided to sound McQueen out, to see if he could get any encouragement. Steve told Norris he had "a nice personality. And you never know, the camera may like you." Norris aimed to find out whether this was true.

In order to pursue this new goal, Norris had to make a big jump. "I was thirty-four years old with a wife and two sons to support," he told the Detroit *News*. "I had seven successful schools in the Los Angeles area and had been world karate champion for six years in a row. But I was bored. I wanted a change." So Norris sold his chain of karate schools and began going to acting school on the G.I. Bill. Steve McQueen recommended Estelle Harmon as a coach and Norris took the advice.

How did Dianne "the worrier" feel about all this? "I wasn't worried," she said. "I knew he'd go straight to the top. In karate he won every award there was to win two or three times, and I knew he'd work as hard as he could to be the best he could be." And he surely did, but this was a whole new world for Norris, a man used to being on top of every situation he found himself in.

Norris, though a public figure, had never really tried to open up in front of people before. He had performed in the competitive arena as well as in the choreographed acrobatic displays that he and his brother Aaron had taken on tour, but that wasn't acting. That was something he knew plenty about—karate. His knowledge of the theatrical arts was somewhat less extensive. "When

I set out to be an actor I had no experience," he told the Detroit *News*. "I mean none."

"I'd never even done anything close to acting," he confessed to Truman. "Not even a high school play. So I walk into Estelle Harmon's acting class. And the first thing they do is they grab another actor and you go into a room to rehearse a scene and walk out in front of the whole class to play it. So I walk in there and the first thing she does is to introduce me to the class as 'Chuck Norris, world karate champion.' And I go, 'Oh, no. I wish she hadn't said that.' So anyway, this girl and I do a scene in front of the class. Afterwards Estelle came up to me and said, 'You know, for an athlete, you're the stiffest person I've ever seen in my whole life.' And I said, 'You know, I've never been so scared in my whole life.'

"The insecurity of doing something totally new in your life, especially when you're in your thirties, is enormous. Once I sold my schools, I was studying eight hours per day and I was lucky that it was on the G.I. Bill, because I didn't have any money. I was doing that for six or seven months when I got the kick-boxing league going. So I was bouncing back and forth between the two of those. Finally, after I'd been studying for about two years, *Breaker! Breaker!* came in."

5

*B*reaker! *Breaker!* was the first film to actually star Chuck Norris. Shot over the course of eleven days in 1976, its budget was under half a million dollars. Norris told the Los Angeles *Times* that his share of the pie was $5,000 and went on to describe it as "a down-home kind of movie" and, incidentally, the one that has remained his dad's favorite. In it, Norris played the role of J.D. Dawes.

Dawes is a long-haul trucker who works out of central California to supplement the meager income he gets as a karate teacher. (One imagines that this role came fairly easily to Norris.) J.D.'s little brother, Billy, is making his very first solo run in J.D.'s truck when he runs into trouble. It seems that a psychotic cult leader named Judge Trimmings (played to the hilt by veteran character actor George Murdock) has set up camp in an obscure ghost town in the area. He and his followers had petitioned the state to grant them a city charter and when Jerry Brown complied they dubbed their haven Texas City.

Texas City has precious little industry to support it. There's a junk yard run by a hillbilly
hairboy and his half-wit brother; a diner that
charges out-of-towners outrageous prices for
contaminated pilchard sandwiches; and a bar
done up as some kind of jumbo dollhouse that's
staffed by an alcoholic party-girl whose make-up
technique must have been borrowed from Bozo.
Not that there are any customers to estrange; the
only guy who's ever seen in there is the Judge,
and at the pace he sucks down those Nyquil
Stingers it's unlikely that he can perceive anything too clearly.

However, the Judge always does manage to see
to it that his own malignant brand of justice is
served. Anyone unlucky enough to stumble
across Texas City gets thrown in jail and hung
with heavy fines, and truckers often have their
cargos and/or rigs confiscated or hijacked. The
profits from this scam keep the town thriving and
everybody happy. All the townies, anyway—a
group that includes neither of the Dawes boys.

After he realizes that Billy has fallen afoul of
something, J.D. begins making inquiries and is
repeatedly told that Texas City is the likely
source of any trouble. Setting off in his snazzy
make-out van, J.D. eventually gets to the town
after a run-in with some moonshining hillbillies
who shoot up his radiator. For lack of anything
better to do, he starts nosing around town while
his van's being "fixed" and, after asking a few
questions, gets arrested for "willfully avoiding a
speedtrap." As many a tough guy was to learn

over the next decade, however, no character portrayed by Norris is easy to hold. Much scrapping occurs.

Breaker! Breaker! also features: a waitress named Arlene with whom J.D. shacks up in his van; adequately brutal treatment of Billy to justify the carnage that J.D. wreaks on Texas City's leading citizens; and a climactic scene with eighteen-wheel trucks reducing the town to matchsticks. Nevertheless, J.D.'s other profession, as a karate sensei, gives Norris the opportunity to deliver the following speech:

"Meditation is essential to martial-arts training," J.D. intones. "It is imperative that you develop yourself not only physically, but mentally and spiritually as well. To meditate, you must concentrate on what we call the third eye. Close your eyes. As you're focusing, you'll notice that it becomes brighter and brighter. Your total concentration is on the third eye." Can you imagine those lines occurring in any of the other CB or trucker movies that were so prevalent around the time of *Breaker! Breaker!*'s release? No way, good buddy.

Amidst the wealth of trucker movies coming out at that time, little effort was made to point out *Breaker! Breaker!*'s obvious differences from the pack. "When they released it, they didn't promote it as a Chuck Norris movie," Norris complained to James Truman. "They promoted it as a CB movie. When it first came out it wasn't doing any business, but then the word got out that it had some good karate in it. It picked up momentum from that, so it actually made more money a week or two after release than it did the week it came out. But it still didn't promote me. I did it, but it didn't launch my career."

Breaker! Breaker! did end up being quite financially successful, however. A recent issue of the Los Angeles *Times* reported that it had grossed $12 million, and that ain't hay. Unfortunately, Norris didn't have a percentage of the take. After the film was wrapped up, he returned his concentration to the study of acting, this time with private instruction from Zina Provendie.

In a recent interview, Provendie told *Spin*: "The problem with him was that he was so gentle he just couldn't show hate for a person. He had no intensity, no bite. We worked on trying to bring that out in him. I remember I told him a story that I'd heard about a school teacher who wanted to punish a pupil and told the rest of the class not to send him a Valentine's Day card. When I mentioned this to Chuck he got livid. The idea of cruelty to children upset him so much that he finally got the edge." This was neither natural nor easy for Norris.

"People don't realize how difficult acting is," Norris said to Truman. "I had no idea how hard it could be trying to maintain a character. Especially with me, because I'm a very controlled individual. My life is very controlled. From years and years of martial-arts training I've really learned to develop control of myself. In film, of course, you have to let something come out on the screen. Most of that comes through my eyes.

My face may be bland, but my eyes tell the story. It was funny, when I was fighting, my opponents could always tell when I was about ready to stomp them, from my eyes. I didn't even know what it was. Like my kids would always know when to stop clowning around. And I'd never say anything. They'd just look at my eyes. The hardest part of acting for me was to relax totally in front of the camera and allow my emotions to show."

"It was a challenge after karate," Norris went on. "It was kind of scary, wondering whether you can do it or not. You just have to maintain a positive mental outlook and visualize yourself doing it, making it. Persistence pays off, it really does. If you persist long enough, inevitably, the goal you've set for yourself will materialize.

"McQueen always told me, 'Make the character as close to yourself as you can. Put as much of yourself, Chuck Norris, into him as you can.'" To *The New York Times,* he added, "I'm not trying to be Dustin Hoffman. I just want to project a strong positive hero image on the screen." Ever since he'd been a boy growing up in Oklahoma, his ideal had been John Wayne, and Norris remained such a fan that when he heard the Duke himself would be attending a private screening of *The Cowboys,* he pulled every string he knew to get an invitation. Wayne was then, and is still, the exact representation of what Norris wants his image on the screen to be.

"What I most admired about John Wayne," he wrote in the introduction to *Toughen Up,* "was the unity of his beliefs in real life and the image he portrayed in the movies. I am working for the same strong America that John Wayne worked for. He believed in his country. He saw its faults, but he also saw its virtues. He knew that any nation is only as good as its people, and I agree."

Saying to Truman that the martial-arts world "is built around positive feelings," Norris has long been known for the enormous amount of time he'll spend speaking to young people at high schools or karate demonstrations. He continued doing this even as his film career began taking more of his time and the message he preached was of "the two paths you can choose to follow. One is positive, one is negative. On the negative path you feel you haven't got a chance. You think nothing good will happen, and you'll be tempted to want to escape by getting drunk or high or violent. This results in self-fulfilling failure. On the positive path, you don't have to wait for things to happen to you. You make them happen. By setting goals and working hard to achieve them—no matter how long it takes—you can succeed. There is really no other way."

"I think we all have our crosses to bear," he told Truman. "We've all had things to overcome in our lives. We've all had obstacles to overcome. And that's what I want my movies to be about —facing these obstacles, dealing with them head-on and overcoming them. People can relate that to their own lives and what they have to face. Losing at anything can be a terrible thing, but

Chuck Norris, the young world karate champion. (Photo courtesy AP/Wide World Photos)

Chuck closes in. (Photo courtesy Russell Turiak)

Chuck's kicking power has yet to be equalled. (Photos courtesy Russell Turiak)

In *Return of the Dragon,* Chuck and Bruce Lee were enemies. In real life, they were friends.

Slaughter in San Francisco—the last time Chuck was vanquished. (Photos courtesy The Memory Shop)

In *Good Guys Wear Black*, John T. Booker sets out to avenge his men. (Photo courtesy The Memory Shop)

A Force of One featured an amazing bout between Norris and real-life champ, Bill Wallace. (Photo courtesy The Lester Glassner Collection)

In *The Octagon*, Chuck must track down his brother. (Photo courtesy Neal Peters)

But there's still time for a rendezvous with the deadly Carol Bagsadarian...

...before the armed showdown takes place. (Photos courtesy The Lester Glassner Collection)

Chuck was on top of the world with four hits in a row. (Photo courtesy AP/Wide World Photos)

In *An Eye for an Eye*, his last straight "chop-socky" role, Chuck must take on a living mountain—Professor Toru Tanaka. (Photo courtesy The Lester Glassner Collection)

you reverse the negative side of the loss and turn
it into positive. Like I did in karate. You think,
'He beat me in a certain way and no one will ever
beat me in that way again.' So that loss becomes
a learning experience. I know a lot of black belts
who have gone to psychiatrists because they lost.
They couldn't handle it." Norris can handle just
about anything, though, and that's good. Because a wave of apathy was about all that greeted
him after the release of *Breaker! Breaker!*

The film was not reviewed extensively, and the
few reviews that did appear were not overly com-
plimentary. Although there had been solid action at the box office, Norris's phone was not
exactly ringing off the hook with offers of more
starring roles. In fact, he got no offers at all.
"Everyone kept saying, 'But Chuck, you're an
athlete, not an actor,'" he told *The New York
Times.* "I had to initiate everything myself." He
worked on a script, in close collaboration with a
friend. When it was finished (and when he wasn't
busy with acting school or the kick-boxing
league) he began taking the script around town,
looking for a producer and a deal.

6

The name of Norris's script was *Good Guys Wear Black*. The idea for the film had come to him even before the *Breaker! Breaker!* project. After fooling around with it solo for a while, he'd hooked up with an old friend and gotten him to knock together a proper screenplay. Briefcase in hand, Norris began hustling every independent producer he could find. He was sure he was too much of an outsider to sell the idea to any of the cliquish major studios, but was equally certain that a prize-winning package could be put together by someone with a million dollars and the right connections. His odyssey was a long one.

For two years Norris toured big offices, small offices, and in-between offices, hoping for just one nod of encouragement. But encouragement was not forthcoming. "They kept asking, 'Why will this movie make money, Chuck?' " he recalled to the Detroit *News*. "I kept answering, 'Because it has a lot of action.' " This was not the answer producers were looking for. They would throw open the current issue of *Variety* and wave the ad pages in his face, pointing out that all the other pictures had "a lot of action." Hell, every picture had "a lot of action."

This became a familiar refrain, but stoicly, Norris continued to make the rounds, day by day, visiting anyone he deemed potentially capable of packaging his concept. Up and down he went, until he figured he'd just about exhausted the supply of able-bodied producers in Greater Los Angeles (a feat comparable to Paul Bunyan draining a Great Lake with a straw). With the list of remaining possibilities now shorter than a poodle's temper, he was struck by inspiration in the night. Lying in bed at home in the wee hours immediately preceding yet another interview, he was replaying all the previous rejections in his mind, trying to come up with a new approach. Then it hit him—while he was nowhere near famous in the film industry, he was definitely a big gun in the world of martial arts. Why not try playing that angle?

The next afternoon he had a meeting with a young upstart producer named Michael Leone. Norris gave Leone the script and launched into his standard rap about who he was, what he had in mind and so on. He played out the same old line, but this time, when Leone leaned forward and asked, "Chuck, why will this movie make money?" Norris was ready.

"Well," he said, "there are over four million people seriously practicing karate in America today. I was the world middleweight karate champion for six years running, and I can guarantee you that every single one of them knows who I am. Regardless of anyone else, if only half of them go to see the movie, at three bucks a ticket, you'll have a six-million-dollar gross on an investment of one million." This made a lot of good sense to Leone and, after carefully examining the script, he raised the million dollars Norris reckoned the project would cost. It turned out to be a good move.

In *Good Guys Wear Black* (sometimes referred to as the first official Chuck Norris film), Norris portrays an ex-Army commando named John T. Booker. During the Vietnam War, Booker had been the commander of an elite secret squadron of special commandos called the Black Tigers. As the war is winding down and peace negotiations with the Viet Cong are under way, Booker and the Tigers are called up for one last mission. Apparently there's a POW camp in which all of the CIA operatives captured during the conflict are being held. Unless these men are moved out within forty-eight hours, the entire population of the camp will be summarily executed. While not eager to be the last casualties in the war, the Black Tigers do take off for the action and are transported by chopper to a spot supposedly near the camp.

After killing a few sentries with oriental throwing stars, the group enters the camp and prepares to liberate the prisoners. Oddly, the first couple of huts they come to are empty. Then, when they blow up one of the compound's central buildings, all hell breaks loose. Numberless spotlights blaze into life simultaneously, auto-matic-weapon fire opens from all sides, and a flood of North Vietnamese regulars appears. The Black Tigers are routed and their ranks deci-mated. To add insult to injury, when they go to reconnoiter with the helicopter that's supposed to carry them out, it never shows.

A hard-ass from the word go, Booker is able to save five of his men and march them out of the jungle. The march takes three weeks, and after-ward he spends two months in a military hospital being debriefed. There he's told that the Viet Cong cracked the Black Tigers' security and then shot down the choppers. By the time he is ready to be released the war has ended and he decides to accept their explanations and to leave the war behind him.

Five years later Booker has gotten his PhD in Political Science and is teaching college courses on the war in which he'd fought. One day he's visited by an attractive young investigative re-porter who's working on a story about the Black Tigers. She heard some loose talk at a Washing-ton party about the unit having been sold down the river to the Cong by American politicos and she wants to know his story. The morning after they shack up, Booker receives a visit from his old CIA contact, Murray Saunders (played by Lloyd Hanes). Murray, too, has the Black Tigers on his mind, since it seems like everyone as-sociated with their last operation is being exter-minated.

What follows is a fairly wordy film, dealing

with the seedy side of post-Watergate politics. There is plenty of action (notably a very 007-ish chase sequence involving a snow-suited assassin, a ski jump, a motorcycle, and some heavy-duty leaping), but there are also some very drawn-out passages in which the ethics of governing are discussed at great length. James Franciscus is suitably slimy as a professional political climber and Dana *(S.W.A.T.)* Andrews shines as an alcoholically over-the-hill aide-de-camp. The best scene, however, is played by Jim *(Gilligan's Island)* Backus. In it, he's a pompous doorman in an opulently epauletted admiral's uniform who gets bullied by Booker and Saunders.

Norris, as Booker, is something less than transcendent. As he readily admits.

"I was surrounded by all these experienced actors like Jim Backus and Dana Andrews," he said to the St. Louis *Post Dispatch.* "And I had all these endless dialogue scenes. I was no good at dialogue." He told *Moviegoer* that he felt like a white belt fighting in a black-belt competition. All he could do was fight for his life and hold on.

Back in the real world, however, Norris was able to do much more than that, and he toured the country extensively in order to promote the film. He moved from town to town as the film opened, talking to newspapers, radio personalities, television variety-show hosts, anybody he thought might help plug the film.

Similar mountain-to-Mohammed tactics were used by the distribution company when theaters balked at running a film with an unknown headliner. "Four-walling it," the distributor, American Cinema, would take over the operation from the theater owner for a fixed per-week fee. They would also assume responsibility for all the bills and receipts. The owner would get $3,000 for the week and American Cinema would win or lose depending on what kind of business they could drum up. They almost always won and Norris remembers their record for one theater/one week profit being in the neighborhood of $20,000. In its first year, *Good Guys Wear Black* grossed $19 million dollars. This time around, Norris reportedly had a piece of the action.

Not that he was all that thrilled with the action he saw on the screen. "The first time I saw myself in *Good Guys Wear Black*," he told the Detroit *News*, "I felt fine about it. After the third or fourth viewing, though, I got so depressed I called Steve McQueen and told him, 'Steve, after this I'll never work again.' He said, 'Nah, it's not that bad. You just talk too much. There's too much dialogue. Let the character actors lay out the plot. Then, when there's something important to say, you say it, and people will listen. Anyway, you'll get better as an actor. You should have seen me in *The Blob*.' " McQueen specifically lambasted him for a scene in which Norris had a twelve-page monologue directed at Franciscus about the morality of the Vietnam War. He told Norris that Booker was "verbalizing a lot that we already know. It's not so much being an actor as projecting a presence."

When Norris made some further desultory

noises about his performance, *Moviegoer* reports that McQueen exploded and chided him for "teaching this philosophy all these years about how you can achieve anything you set your mind on" and then turning hypocritical when his own chips were down. This was powerful stuff and it gave Norris the kick in the pants he deserved. He had enormous respect for McQueen (he once said that after John Wayne, Steve was his favorite actor) and wouldn't soon grouse about his lot again.

Not surprisingly, reviewers were unkind. Rather than deal with the rather sophisticated political ramifications of *Good Guys,* they contented themselves by handling it as just another "chop socky" film. The fact that *Good Guys* had twenty times as much plot as any of the kung-fu potboilers being churned out in Hong Kong moved the critics not a whit. They didn't care that Norris had taken pains to give the movie's action a feel far different from the cheaply produced fare to which it was often compared.

"In my fight scenes, I always ask myself what I would do in a real situation like this," Norris explained to the St. Louis *Post Dispatch.* "That's if I couldn't get out of it, of course. And because they film so spectacularly, especially in slow motion, there are more kicks in *Good Guys* than a martial artist would normally use, but it's important to me that the audience feels emotionally involved with my character. They're not just watching a lot of fights. What Bruce Lee and I tried to demonstrate is that there's always a market for a hero. So many of the top stars play anti-heros these days. When I was growing up, stars like John Wayne and Gary Cooper stood for ideals. My characters do too."

You couldn't really take the papers to task for assuming *Good Guys Wear Black* was "chop socky" fare, however. The ads for the thing read, "He fought to the death with Bruce Lee. He's fighting mad. Chuck Norris is John T. Booker and Booker is fighting mad." Still, you had to wonder if the critics had seen the whole movie.

Chastised by some papers for involving himself with films that made violence look like an attractive proposition, Norris explained to *The New York Times* that his characters "don't initiate violence. They retaliate. In my films I'm forced into a situation that I must cope with. Even though I have to do it in a violent way, I think the audience understands the motivation behind it. My films deal with certain positive things and I think a lot of people are tired of depressing, boring films. I think they like to feel good at the end of a film." Judging by his box-office figures, the people agreed. Furthermore, American Cinema agreed with the people and after Norris was sufficiently rested from his exhausting promotional tour, work began on his next feature.

In *A Force of One,* Norris plays a tournament karate champion, Matt Logan, who's based in the fictional town of Santa Madre, California. Shot in and around Santa Monica, the film deals with a drug epidemic that's gripping the quiet coastal city of Santa Madre. In the opening sequence two cops watch a drug dealer ride a skateboard across town to a sporting goods store where he makes a drop and a pickup. Figuring to go on a little "hunting expedition without a license," the pair return that night, only to be dispatched by a dark-clothed figure who seems to know quite a bit about "the art of the empty hand."

The bodies are hauled out of the bay the next day, and it's the coroner's verdict that their windpipes were hit so hard they drowned in blood. "What could have done such a thing?" the police ask. "Maybe it's one of those karate weirdos," someone suggests. The very idea causes snickers throughout the room. The Captain thinks there might be something to it, though, and he asks Matt to step in and give his people some training. Logan refuses at first, but after Officer Mandy Rust (played by a very oddly coiffed Jennifer O'Neill) shows him some of the horrors that drugs are responsible for, he changes his tune.

When more members of the narcotics squad are iced, everybody gets a lot more serious about their martial-arts training and they set out, in earnest, to track down "The Karate Killer." Unfortunately for them, a big martial-arts tournament is being held and the town is filled to bursting with folks who possess the know-how to have committed the crimes. Logan, meanwhile, is getting ready for his big match with an old Army buddy, played by Bill "Superfoot" Wallace.

Their full-contact match is the film's best battle. But first, Logan begins to really put his all into the police work because his adopted son was killed by the drug ring. What turns up is solid evidence of police corruption, and a chase through the Santa Monica Mountains ends with some satisfying bone-crunching.

Especially noteworthy in *A Force of One* are Ron *(Superfly)* O'Neal in a change of pace role (from pimp to cop), a cameo appearance by *Deep Throat*'s Harry Reems (as a clerk in the evidence room at police headquarters, and the powerful presence of Bill Wallace. Wallace is a past world karate champion (he, also, went undefeated for six years), a gifted teacher (with a series of best-selling instructional and fight video cassettes on the market), and one of the people whose name comes up whenever fans try to determine who was the greatest karate fighter of all time (Norris, naturally, is another oft-mentioned name). Wallace has appeared in numerous kung-fu flicks, often as a heavy, and his involvement with film began when he signed on as John Belushi's personal bodyguard for the Blues Brothers Tour. Wallace's technique, as heavily reliant on kicks as Norris's own, is astounding to watch, and the fight between the two is one of filmdom's best.

When *A Force of One* was released, Norris again took to the road to promote it. Thankfully, he didn't have to work at it quite so hard this time around. People remembered *Good Guys Wear Black,* and its financial success had been well reported throughout the industry. Still, many local distributors considered *Good Guys* to have been a fluke, so American Cinema once more had their work cut out for them. And once more they succeeded admirably. Shot for a cost of $2.5 million, *A Force of One* eventually took in almost $25 million. The critics even had a few kind words for it.

The Washington *Post* grudgingly admitted that Norris was "a sincere B-movie straight arrow," and when you think about what he wanted as a screen image, well, that's not too far off the mark. As he told *Moviegoer,* "I was aware of my lack of experience as an actor, so I decided that I would create a character on the screen that people would like—one that was fairly similar to me, so I could get in as much realism as possible, but mostly the character that I would want to be seen as. I'm more or less a loner, a man who has strong principles, and I do my utmost to succeed in whatever I'm doing—although I'm more subtle in real life than I am in movies."

"I was very happy with *A Force of One,*" Norris wrote in *Toughen Up.* "The kids of America really loved it. One of the reasons they did was a fight scene between my character and a pimp. It was the easiest fight scene in the film, but it got the biggest response because it was a classic confrontation between good and evil. It showed, I think, the need people have today to see heros on the screen. The time has passed for the anti-hero; for the actor whose image is not really good, not really bad, sort of gray. People want a fellow who can fight evil and win. The kids need it." And

Norris was not averse to knocking the hell out of evil.

The Octagon was Norris's next vehicle. His character, a retired karate fighter named Scott James, is so close to *A Force of One*'s Matt Logan that some writers called it a sequel to the earlier film, even though the story was in no way similar.

Scott James is a man with a mysterious past. He was raised, for reasons unknown, by a martial-arts master in a wild area of Japan. His "brother" in this strange family was a Japanese lad his own age named Seikura. The boys were constantly together and they were taught all of their foster dad's fighting secrets. Everything goes pretty swimmingly until the boys come of age, at which point Seikura, in a burst of egoism, proves to be such a bad loser that he gets kicked out of camp. The old man goes so far as to tell Scott that Seikura is now "his lifelong enemy." Scott doesn't quite understand the logic of this, but he respects his elders and so accepts this statement as the truth.

Years later Scott becomes romantically involved with a young ballerina. In the wake of a terrorist attack, the ballerina and all her family are slaughtered by what appear to be ninja. The ninja were a sect of silent Japanese assassins active during that country's feudal period. They have not existed for hundreds of years, even though some of their weapons techniques are still taught at the highest level of study at the Katori Shinto Ryu school. Scott knows intellectually that they cannot exist, but he's seen and fought with what certainly appeared to be ninja. An inner voice tells him that only Seikura could be behind these black-garbed killers.

Interwoven with this tale of Scott's personal development (told through numerous flashbacks and voice-overs) is one about a ninja training camp for international terrorists located in an obscure outpost somewhere in Central America. Numerous personal affronts are dealt to Scott before he feels compelled to really kick ass, but he eventually hands severe whuppings to every man-jack that crosses his path. Four at a time, five at a time, armed, unarmed, he doesn't discriminate. The big climax of the film is a sword fight in the midst of a blazing inferno, and while the plot's a little snaky for mere mortals to follow, the action's virtually nonstop.

Still, the critics were not quite satisfied. *People* described his characterization of Scott as "too nice—like a Redford of the martial arts." Oddly, though, the movie picked up good notices from *New York*, which reported that Norris was "certainly impressive in action," adding that, "movies like *The Octagon* glory in something genuine —a love of fighting and a love of prowess, two qualities dependably popular the world over. If international mass culture has a bedrock, this is it." Very true.

This time around, the concept that Norris was something of a flash in the pan was no longer in fashion, so theaters booked *The Octagon* even before it was finished filming. With a budget of

$4 million, *The Octagon* reportedly took in over $18 million and American Cinema, which had had just one salaried employee when it first decided to back *Good Guys Wear Black*, now had 180. Due, in large part, to the success of Norris's three hits, the company was now at the stage where it could be called "a mini major." Norris, however, was at the stage where he needed a major major to handle him, and with *The Octagon* in the can, he once more headed off for bigger pastures.

7

The production company Norris picked for his next project was Avco Embassy, a fairly large outfit of high standing in the film community. Although Avco Embassy was not one of the top-line major studios, it was capitalized far in excess of American Cinema and had a proven track record. Norris wanted no part of the taxing promotional gyrations that his earliest films had required. He felt sure that Avco Embassy was up to the task of his latest project—a film called *An Eye for an Eye*.

With its harsh, Biblical title, *An Eye for an Eye* presented Norris in the role of Sean Kane, a San Francisco narcotics cop. It was directed by Steve Carver, a disciple of B-movie guru Roger Corman, and had a budget of $4 million. As the film opens, Kane and his partner are sitting in a car, apparently on some kind of stakeout. (Kane is bugged because his partner, Dave Pierce, is blowing smoke in his face, so the first line Norris utters is, "Goddamn shit.") The object of the pair's vigil finally hoves into view and they trail him into a wino hotel. The guy indicates to the cops that he can't talk to them there, and that they should meet him outside for a pow-wow.

Kane and Pierce follow the pigeon through the rain to an empty parking lot. When they get there, however, their bird has flown. Sensing trouble, they pull their guns, but it's too late. Automatic weapons open up on them from behind parked autos. Pierce is hit right away, but Kane manages to dodge. The gunsels jump in their cars to take off, but Kane succeeds in pegging a driver before he can exit the lot. The car hits a wall and is enveloped in a ball of flames. Unfortunately, this fireball also contains the wounded Officer Pierce.

Blocked by the blazing inferno, Kane can only watch helplessly as Pierce is fried to a cinder. There's nothing he can do but listen to his partner's agonized screams, so he takes off after some gunmen who'd fled on foot. He shoots one and pursues the other into the hotel they'd just left. After a foot chase that combines elements of both suspense and comedy, Kane corners the rat. Obviously pissed, he throws down his gun and punches the guy so hard he goes flying through the nth-story window. Kane's superior officer, Captain Stevens (portrayed by Richard *Shaft* Roundtree) appears almost immediately and demands to know, "What the hell happened?" Later, Kane speculates that the pair was set up. Stevens says this is a virtual impossibility and reprimands Kane for knocking that clown through the window. Kane hands in his gun and badge, vowing to take care of it by himself.

Kane is next shown working out and swallowing pounds of vitamins. We learn that Pierce's girl friend, Linda Chan, is a TV reporter who's been doing a series on drugs and drug-smuggling in the San Francisco area. After some wailing bagpipe tunes at Pierce's funeral we discover that Linda's father, James, was Kane's sensei. Now James is concentrating on his meditation and gardening, and Linda says he will never leave his hilltop home across the bay. Linda vows that she'll soon have heads rolling with her televised investigative journalism, however, and that Pierce's death will not go unavenged.

Linda doesn't look quite so confident when we next see her. In fact, she's terrified, and is being chased through a BART (Bay Area Rapid Transit) station by a giant, played by Professor Toru Tanaka. As wrestling fans know, Tanaka is no pansy. A towering mountain of milk-fed beef, the Professor was the archetypal oriental bad guy of Wrestling's Golden Quarter Century (1945–1970). Unlike some of his rivals, who used ersatz "joodoo" moves or "koroty" chops to humble challengers, Tanaka actually knew what he was doing. A first-degree black belt in Akido and Master status in Tai Chi Chu'an surely attest to that. Wielded by the Professor, fists the size of small dogs carry quite a load, and the scenes of him disrupting pedestrian traffic in the BART station are choice.

Anyhow, when Linda thinks she's put enough distance between herself and Tanaka, she calls Kane and says she's got the goods on the drug ring. Not surprisingly, by the time Kane gets to her it's too late. The rest of the film revolves around his revenge.

For the first time, Norris's character acts vicious. Not content with stopping the bad guys in *An Eye for an Eye,* he goes out of his way to make sure he kills them. Backs snap like kindling, as Kane and his former teacher, James (portrayed by the awesome Japanese-American character actor Mako), go on a rampage of retaliatory violence against the drug-smugglers and their lackeys. The climactic fight scene between Tanaka and Kane is, perhaps, not the monster it could have been, but the general high level of carnage should keep most fans happy. Another treat is Christopher Lee's portrayal of the autocratic television network owner. This is a nice change of pace for viewers used to seeing him play only evil roles in the films that poured out of England's Hammer Studios. In all, a good flick. Would that the critics had thought the same.

The Washington *Post* groused that Norris looked like "Hans Brinker, grown up to be a palooka, because of the Little Dutch Boy haircut that crowns his thick, long-jawed, mournful mug." They didn't like the film either, and felt that Richard Roundtree, if anyone, should have received top billing. *The New York Times* whined that the fight scenes looked "phony," and even *People* labeled it as "insidious Hollywood poppycock." *Variety,* however, noted that Norris's "acting is improving and his balletic fighting and kicking skills remain tops in the field. He is the current champ of the chop socky genre." That was pretty much on the mark, but the very fact that it was accurate was a problem. See, Norris didn't want to be King of Chop Socky. He never had, ad campaigns like "Chuck Norris doesn't need a weapon . . . he is a weapon!" notwithstanding.

"The Weapon" felt cramped by the confines of the martial-arts ghetto his films were always being shunted into. Norris didn't really care if, as the Chicago *Tribune* maintained, "the state of the martial-arts movie has been languishing ever since the death of Bruce Lee." Let it languish! If a guy like the acrobatic Jackie Chan (sometimes called "The Korean Burt Reynolds") wanted to be heir-apparent to the chop socky kingdom of Lee, let him. With five successful feature films under his belt, Norris wanted to try something a bit different—something like the project his younger brother, Aaron, had in mind.

Aaron was thinking of a film with science-fiction overtones to it, a film that would show his big bro not just as a fighter, but as a lover as well. In short, a film like the one Aaron got associate producer's credit for when Columbia decided to make *Silent Rage*. In his first film for a major studio (Columbia is a long way from American Cinema), Norris plays Sheriff Dan Stevens, a tough lawman based in a small town in the American Southwest.

As the film opens, we witness a brutal murder by a psychotic named John Kirby who's driven to violence by the shrill shrieks of children playing. Pumped full of lead and soundly thrashed by Stevens, Kirby still seems to be alive when the ambulance arrives to cart him off. The next time we see Kirby he has seemingly expired on the table in a hospital that's part of a nearby genetic research clinic. After some hot ethical debating, the three doctors standing at Kirby's bed decide to pump him full of a secret chemical called Mitogen 35 . . . and the plot thickens.

Stevens discovers that Kirby's psychiatrist is the brother of an old flame of his named Allison Halman and, when the two are reunited, the juices flow. At about the same time, the town is visited by a cadre of porky motorcycle badasses who proceed to give Stevens and his deputy Charlie (a really great character played by Steven Furst, best known as "Flounder" from the film *Animal House*) a hard time.

Stevens wipes up a bar with about a dozen of the cyclists while Charlie sits outside in the patrol car rhapsodizing about the incredible breasts a biker mama just flashed at him. "You know, I may be in love," Charlie muses while Stevens stomps rump a few feet away. "They were the biggest things I've ever seen and they had tattoos on them. I may just go right back in there and ask her for a date."

Needless to say, the tryst never materializes and Stevens and Charlie soon have their hands full of something else entirely. It seems that the injection of Mitogen 35 has not just brought Kirby back to life, it's given him superhuman strength and a bodily system that heals any wound almost immediately. Kirby soon takes care of everybody he feels has wronged him, and then goes after the ones he thinks *might* harm him. Stevens follows a trail of bodies to the creature's lair and a donnybrook ensues.

Interwoven with this basic story is one subplot about medical ethics, another about Charlie's good-natured buffoonery, and yet another about the way Stevens manages the flow of hormones through his system when he rubs up against a woman. It was a distinctly different type of film from anything Norris had made before.

Technically, the production values afforded the picture by Columbia gave it a better "look" on the screen than some of its predecessors (notably *A Force of One,* which according to one reviewer appeared to have been mishandled at the lab); and there were advances in other areas as well. The script was by far Norris's best yet. The acting of his fellow performers (especially the roly-poly Furst) was of the highest caliber. There was even what *People* called "a convincing love interest." Some critics even liked it. But wouldn't you know it? His fans disagreed.

For one thing, *Silent Rage* was the first film to have what Norris called "a tussle with a female co-star," and this particular brand of derring-do ruffled the feathers of many of his long-time fans. Furthermore, while the ads screamed: "SCIENCE CREATED IT . . . NOW CHUCK NORRIS MUST DESTROY IT!" as far as many veteran Norris-watchers were concerned, he didn't destroy it enough. "My audiences don't like me domesticated," he told the Los Angeles

Times. "They want me to be a free spirit. They tell me. They write me letters. They tell my fan club. A lot of kids go to see my movies and they don't like to see me in steamy stuff."

Just how "steamy" Norris's moments with actress Toni Kalem were is open to debate. As *The New York Times* reported, "In the scene where Mr. Norris and Miss Kalem make love, Mr. Norris is shirtless more often than Miss Kalem, which is probably a first." The fans didn't go for it, either, so Norris admitted that he didn't really think of himself as a romantic anyway and vowed to get back on the right track immediately.

Forced Vengeance, produced by MGM/Columbia, was the result of Norris's decision to mollify his old crew. It certainly should have done that—in spades. Norris's character this time is named Josh Randall. Based in Hong Kong as members of the Special Forces, Randall and a large pal named Leroy Nicely had once gotten drunk and busted the hell out of a casino called the Lucky Dragon. The owner of the Dragon was an expatriot American named Sam Paschal (played here by the excellent David Opatoshi). Sam knew an amazing fighting machine when he saw one, and he hired Randall as head of security the second his tour of duty was finished. Satisfied with this arrangement, Randall took up residence on a houseboat, bought a huge wardrobe of Western-style togs (even his tuxedo has cowboy-style stitching), and became a good friend of the entire Paschal clan.

When the story opens (after an amazingly

beautiful title sequence, featuring a slow-motion fight shot in front of a blazing red neon backdrop), all is not well at the Lucky Dragon. Sam has been retired for a few years and in his absence the casino has not thrived. All he really wants now is to tend his garden. Management of the casino has been left up to his son, David. Theoretically, a piece of the management is also handled by Sam's daughter, Joy, but she is something of a jet-setter and cannot be moved from her exclusive swinging singles condo by anything as mundane as work.

Left to his own devices, David concludes that the Dragon is run in too old-fashioned a manner. When he's approached with a merger proposal by the local syndicate chief, Stan Raimondi (played with simmeringly ugly malevolence by Michael Cavenaugh), he's all for it. Of course, Raimondi's plan stinks, as Sam is quick to point out when he, David, and Randall visit Raimondi's headquarters. The basic deal is that the Lucky Dragon either joins the Osiris "family" or gets put out of business by the company goons. Over David's whinnying protests, Sam tells Raimondi to take his deal and hide it in a dark warm place. And then the bloodbath begins.

Forced Vengeance was, by far, the most violent film Norris had made up to this point. Something evil befalls almost every character and, since some of the characters are wonderfully engaging, the impact of their collective fates is great. By the time Randall has dispatched the pugs that have wronged him and gotten his hands on Mr. Big (with a modicum of assistance from a mysterious police inspector), we're almost ready to strangle the guy ourselves, so thoroughly nasty has Big's every move been. Fortunately, we are once again saved from getting our hands dirty by Norris's nimble footwork.

The amount of anti-personnel damage handed out in *Forced Vengeance* is extensive and it makes for a visually powerful film. This was not the critical consensus. Apart from boosters in the martial-arts publication fraternity who named him "Man of the Year" in *Black Belt* and a charter member of "The Legion of Honor" in *Official Karate,* Norris was virtually without a friend with a pen.

Variety griped that, "For Norris, who has given signs of trying to graduate from the chop socky genre, this is a step backwards." Furthermore, they predicted that if the film (shot in 1982 under the title *Jade Jungle,* then called *Vengeance Is Mine,* and then *Vengeance Force* before the final selection was arrived at) were found by industry-conscious archeologists of the twenty-second century, it would be declared to have dated from the early to mid-Seventies. Gee, that's mean. *People* added that "the plot is rickety with age."

The tenor of these negative comments, however, makes it seem likely that Norris had achieved his stated goal of appeasing the fans he'd upset with *Silent Rage. Time* counted seventeen distinct martial-arts sequences, enough for any connoisseur, one would think. The fans were delighted, but the critics were vicious. Norris felt as if he were caught between the proverbial rock and hard place.

"It's happened," he told James Truman, "that my movies didn't do what I thought they would. I'd ask myself why people didn't like it, but then I'd say, 'Hey—you've got another movie to do. The movie didn't lose money. It didn't make a hundred million dollars, but so what? Cut that out.' The movie business is a very insecure business. You never know if you're going to be employed again. Then there're the critics. They can annihilate you, blast you, make you feel bad. There are so many tough aspects to the business that I didn't know about when I went into it. But these are the challenges, the things you face up against and just see what you can do. I get crucified by the critics every time and I say, 'Gee, well the people liked it.' "

"I still haven't reached what I consider the pinnacle of success," he told the Detroit *News*. "I still haven't honed the basic character to where I want him and I still haven't reached the basic goal I set for myself—to become a big star in action-type films. Sure, I've got a certain following, but there's a long way to go before I'm at the level of a Clint Eastwood or a Burt Reynolds. When and if I reach that place, then we'll see what's next. For now, I'm sticking with the martial-arts movies. As we're able to bring up the budgets, I'm trying to bring up the quality.

"The way I figure it, there are two groups of

people in my business. At one end of the spectrum you have the actors' actors—Dustin Hoffman, Laurence Olivier. Actors people gladly pay to see in anything because they're so talented. At the other end of the spectrum you have the personalities—Clint Eastwood, Burt Reynolds, Charles Bronson. I fit in there somewhere. Now Clint and Burt, they can afford to break away from their known screen personalities. And they don't have to worry if their movies bomb. They're rich. They have enormous power in the business. They'll just go on working. With me, people come to see Chuck Norris because he can handle anything—physically or psychologically. That's what they pay for. If I were to take the part of a gay person, like Christopher Reeve did in *Deathtrap,* I'd be out of work. Just that quick."

Not wishing to be unemployed "just that quick," Norris has yet to accept a gay role, but his next film made the sort of break with the genre he'd been looking for, while keeping his character more than tough enough for his fans.

8

To make his seventh film, Norris went to Orion
Pictures, another of the industry's big guns.
What he had in mind this time was a project
tentatively titled *Last of the Breed*. This film
would take the man's-man character that Norris
had long been developing and place it in its natural surroundings—the mythic West. But this
would not be the West of the nineteenth-century
gunfighter; this would be Texas today. The character would be a Texas Ranger who was maybe
a little old-fashioned but still a distinctly modern
guy. Norris would finally get to play the kind of
role he'd always wanted, a sort of contemporary
version of the John Wayne and Gary Cooper
characters that had galvanized his imagination
back in Oklahoma. The name of the Texas
Ranger was James J. ("Lone Wolf") McQuade,
and eventually it was decided that this should be
the film's moniker as well.

Lone Wolf McQuade opens with the full-
bearded title character standing on a desert bluff
looking through a rifle scope at some men driv-

ing horses through winding sandy passages. On another bluff we can see a group of uniformed policemen preparing to head off the riders. As the police start moving down the slope, the camera pans through the dust and horses, catching the faces of the bandits in portraits reminiscent of *The Wild Bunch* or *The Good, the Bad and the Ugly*. When the first move is made, McQuade takes a rifle from his truck and clips on the scope. It's only then that we can see he's got a badge.

Down below, the police move in. One of them uses a bullhorn to announce that all the rustlers are under arrest. Brandishing guns, the bandits laugh and open fire. Drastically outnumbered, the police are soon flanked and surrounded by the hombres. The fat leader of the bandits (who looks and sounds a lot like the guy in *Treasure of the Sierra Madre* who chastened Humphrey Bogart with the line, "Badges? We don't need no steenking badges!") takes the captured cops, lines them up near the trucks his confederates have brought in to cart off the horses, and prepares to execute them. As he raises his machete to kill the first man, McQuade lifts his rifle and fires a few incendiary rounds into the waiting vehicles. They blow up and the bandits are thrown into confusion. They fire aimlessly until one of them spots McQuade crouching on a mesa some two hundred yards away.

The shooting stops when McQuade's location is determined. Seeing that he seems to be alone, one of the rustlers hoots, "Hey, you should stand up like a man." McQuade complies and doesn't flinch an inch when a potshot thrown at him goes low. He just raises his rifle to his shoulder and blows one of the bandits away. The leader of the gang retaliates by grabbing one of the handcuffed cops, putting a gun to his head, and summarily murdering him. Then he quickly grabs another handcuffed cop (played by Robert Beltran, the young star of *Eating Raoul*), places the gun to his head, and waits.

McQuade stands up. Alone on the mesa with the sun at his back, he looks a lot like the character he worshipped during his youth—the compleat frontiersman. Self-reliant, assured, in charge of his fate, McQuade comes down off his mountain to face the men. They're sure they'll soon be wearing his pelt on their belts and laugh in glee at the thought. But McQuade knows different. He walks up to the head honcho, who looks at him and says, "Once a Texas Ranger knocked my father's teeth out. Would you do that, Texas Ranger?" Apparently interpreting this as a polite request, Chuck obliges the gent and grabs his machine gun in the ensuing confusion.

Later, McQuade, still wearing the same dirty, sweat-encrusted garb in which he'd just fought, is seen attending a retirement ceremony for one of the Rangers. The retiree's name is Dakota (played by veteran Western actor L.Q. Jones) and it seems that he, like McQuade, is a round peg in a square hole. The two are drinking some beer off to the side of the podium after the ceremony when the Captain appears. He knocks the can out of McQuade's hand and tells him to get up to his office. Once there, a lecture ensues.

While acknowledging that McQuade's record for unassisted arrests is exemplary, the Captain declares, "There's a lot more to being a Texas Ranger than making busts." His conception of a Texas Ranger is a model citizen, a pillar of the community, who goes to church, lives clean, and has a loving wife and kids. More to the point, an editorial in the local paper written by a state senator, chairman of the committee that funds the Rangers, has specifically named McQuade as a brutal and out-of-date member of the force. The Captain tells McQuade he's got to have a partner and introduces him to Kayo, the young Ranger who'd had the pistol held to his temple earlier. McQuade lets it be known that he needs a partner like he needs an extra nose and heads home for a little rest and relaxation.

Kayo observes from a distance as McQuade pulls various weapons out of his personal arsenal for some target shooting in his backyard. In a display similar to the target practice that keeps Navy destroyers "in shape," McQuade blows the hell out of his property with a wide assortment of large-barrel guns and explosive ammo. Kayo's impressed. He becomes even more impressed after a little race between his cop car and McQuade's Dodge Ram. Kayo had taken pains to inform McQuade of the police car's super-charged engine, little realizing that McQuade's engine has had the same treatment and then some.

At this stage of the game, subplots start to weave their way through the action. McQuade's estranged wife, Molly (he's still friendly with her; she just couldn't handle a Ranger's working hours) is going to move out of the area. She's lined up a better job elsewhere and she's leaving with their daughter, Sally. McQuade takes Sally riding at the track, where her horse bolts on her. She's saved by a beautiful young widow named Lola Richardson (played by the exotic Nicaraguan beauty, Barbara Carrera).

We are also introduced to Lola's business (and presumably bunk) partner, an arms smuggler named Rawley Wilkes. Wilkes is played to smarmy perfection by David Carradine—an inspired casting choice, as Carradine's greatest fame is for his role as the fugitive martial-arts master, Caine, in ABC's *Kung Fu* television series. According to the Houston *Post,* Carradine (here portraying a guy who's supposed to be the European karate champ, among other things) had it written into his contract that he would not be allowed to lose a karate fight to Norris. They should have let them fight for real!

As the story continues, Sally and her beau witness the hijacking of an arms shipment. Her boyfriend is killed and she's left for dead by the side of the road. This gets McQuade peeved enough to start throwing his weight around, and he leans on all manner of folks (even consenting to the torture of one) in order to crack the case. A peculiarly prescient midget floats in and out of the proceeding, Barbara Carrera remains in-

Chuck Norris at the end of a long day's shooting. (Photo courtesy Frank Edwards, Pictorial Parade, Inc.)

Sheriff Dan Stevens is the only one who can stop the superhuman terror in *Silent Rage*.

Or can he? (Photos courtesy The Lester Glassner Collection)

Two of the precious assets Josh Randall must guard in *Forced Vengeance*.

Randall gets ready to deliver a haymaker. (Photos courtesy The Lester Glassner Collection)

Lone Wolf McQuade—the last of a breed. (Photo courtesy The Lester Glassner Collection)

Barbara Carrera comes between McQuade and his arch rival David Carradine
... (Photo courtesy The Memory Shop)

...but nothing can come between Carrera and McQuade. (Photo courtesy SIPA/ Special Features)

Col. James Braddock is a man with a mission in *Missing in Action*. (Photo courtesy The Lester Glassner Collection)

Braddock brings down a rain of death on the Viet Cong. (Photo courtesy The Memory Shop)

Sergeant Eddie Cusack is the only cop tough enough to crack the *Code of Silence.* (Photo courtesy The Lester Glassner Collection)

With 2,000 rounds per minute at his command, Matt Hunter may just be the man to stop *Invasion USA.* (Photo courtesy The Lester Glassner Collection)

spirationally bra-less throughout the film, McQuade gets a timely assist by a Federal agent named Jackson, and there's plenty of action: armed combat, unarmed combat, explosives, you name it. All in all, a doozy of a flick.

Before the film got a chance to go public, however, Norris had to fight another battle, this time in his real-life guise as all-around nice guy. It seems that the MPAA rating board had taken a look at *Lone Wolf McQuade* and decided that it deserved an "R" rating. This determination was made not because of the scene where McQuade and Lola do a little at-home mud wrestling, but rather because they felt the film was too violent. Orion protested that there really wasn't that much violence in *Lone Wolf,* and, further, what was there was non-gory and almost tame by current standards. When the Board wouldn't buy this line, Orion called in the cavalry—Norris.

Chuck pleaded his case with an impassioned speech in which he defended the movie's action sequences as stylized passages, more in the manner of John Wayne than Leathermask. He also stressed the fact that the film had a positive message for young people. As he told *The New York Times,* "I told them I would never do a movie that I felt was detrimental to kids. I think you can do action movies without getting into strong violence. And you don't take McQuade real serious; he's fun." Norris won the case on appeal, so *Lone Wolf McQuade* (which he actually co-produced with Orion) was unleashed on the world with a "PG" rating. And for once, the popular and critical responses to the film started to converge.

While many of the reviews included slightly catty remarks about the film's numerous cinematographic references to Clint Eastwood, most acknowledged that *Lone Wolf McQuade* was a big step for Norris. Even with a few big fight scenes in which karate was used, there was no way it could be called a kung-fu film, so the "chop socky" sobriquet didn't really fit anymore. Robbed of this easy phrase, critics were nearly forced to admit that Lone Wolf was indeed an action-adventure film pure and simple. Not wanting to do that just yet, they couched all their kind words inside of "second-hand Eastwood" essays.

The Houston *Post* said, "Norris is repeatedly lit and photographed to look like a 1980s version of Clint Eastwood's *Man with No Name.*" *Variety* called McQuade "a sagebrush Dirty Harry" and said that Norris seemed to be "carving a slightly different, less specialized screen persona for himself, more along the lines of Clint Eastwood." *Rolling Stone* said, "Playing an individualistic Texas Ranger in his new film, Norris makes Eastwood look like a paragon of emotion."

There was also praise given without a breath of the hallowed Eastwood name. The Detroit *News* was all atwitter because Norris had grown a beard, "adding a flattering fullness to his face. He's more handsome than the long-jawed fellow of his earlier pictures." *People* called *Lone Wolf*

"Norris's best yet" and good-naturedly sub-
titled it *Night of the Living Die Hard. The New
York Times* likened it to an "old-fashioned Saturday afternoon serial."

Norris seemed excited to think he had finally
broken out of the kung-fu mold. As he told *USA
Today,* "*McQuade* is a transition for me. It's
about a guy who's still a hero, but on a more
aggressive level. I think my audience wants me
to be a little less timid." The newspaper agreed
that Norris's previous heros had seemed "too
slow to rage," and that this film seemed likely to
make him appealing even to folks with no interest in the martial-arts. Of course, as Norris
pointed out for the hundredth time, he had never
intended to be a kung-fu star in the first place.

"If you look at my movies of the past," he
explained to the Houston *Post,* "they've never
really been karate movies or chop socky movies.
I've never wanted to be labelled a 'karate movie
star,' but it's been hard. It's taken me about eight
years to slowly break out of that mold, to break
away from the idea that, 'Oh, if you go see a
Chuck Norris film all you'll see is karate.' I think
cable TV has helped me out tremendously. People are seeing my movies on video and finding
out that they're not just karate movies. Right
now I'm finally getting some good, very well-
written scripts. In the early days, people felt,
'Well, he's just going to do karate movies, so
we've got to write things with karate in them.'
But things have changed. The films I'm making
now have a lot more texture to them. They have

a lot of good acting in them. And the movies themselves are very well done."

"After eight years, people still say to me, 'You know, I haven't seen any of your kung-fu pictures,'" Norris told the L.A. *Times.* "All I can tell them is that 'they're not kung-fu movies. They never were.' That's why I can't do a full-fledged martial-arts movie now." It didn't really seem as if anyone wanted him to do one, either. While the box office on *Silent Rage,* his first "crossover" attempt, had been sluggish, *Lone Wolf McQuade* piled up $15 million worth of receipts in fairly short order. This led *USA Today* to dub him "one of Hollywood's most bankable stars" and they were certainly right on that count. If *Lone Wolf McQuade* marked Norris's tentative first step out of the chop socky ghetto (at least in the critics' eyes), his next brace of films represented a jump of dizzying proportions.

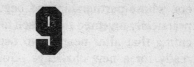

After the well-deserved success of *Lone Wolf McQuade,* Norris once again made the rounds looking for the right production company for his newest project. He was now a verifiable hot ticket, far from the unknown "karate guy" he'd been when he first set out with the *Good Guys Wear Black* script tucked under his arm. His films made money and had been consistently doing so for almost a decade. He had always seen that his work received as much coverage in the press as he could drum up, and now the coverage was finally becoming positive. He was known as a hard worker and family man with no vices at all. He had a reputation as a nice guy who played it straight with all comers. He had a script he wanted to shoot. He was looking for a deal. Enter Cannon Films.

Once a B-movie house churning out cheesy grinders for the drive-in set, Cannon had been going through major changes since 1979. That was the year it was taken over by Menahem Golan and Yoram Globus. This pair of producers, whose partnership had begun in 1960, had practically invented the Israeli film industry. Deciding that after nearly two decades they were ready for a new challenge, Golan and Globus moved to California, bought a controlling interest in Cannon, and immediately set about shaking the place up. They started using Cannon to back prestige films by directors like Cassavetes, Altman, and Wertmuller, as well as such lighter fare as *Bolero, That Championship Season,* and *Lifeforce.* During the 1983–84 season they reportedly set more films into motion than any other company, and it was then that Cannon signed Norris to what is rumored to have been a six-picture, $6 million deal. "They give me the leeway I want," he happily reported to James Truman.

What he had in mind when he first approached Cannon was something very close to his heart— a story dealing with the 2,500 people who were still reported as missing in action from the Vietnam War. The reason this was so important to him is simple—the older of his two brothers, Wieland, had been killed in Vietnam in 1969.

"Wieland was in the Army," Norris told Truman. "He was a little bit older than most when he went in—he was twenty-six—and he was a squadron leader in Vietnam. He was heading up a squad that was on patrol when he stopped the patrol and went on ahead to see if any traps were being set. He wasn't far before he ran into a Viet Cong patrol setting up traps, and when he called back for his men to take cover, the Viet Cong opened up fire on him. That was his first tour. He'd only been there about four months.

"It was an extremely hard blow for the family. Wieland was one of my black belts, one of my instructors . . . he was my best friend. We were very, very close. That made it doubly hard. I was at a karate tournament, judging, when I heard. I was right in the middle of it when I got a call. It was my mother-in-law; she was crying. She told me. At first I had no reaction. I just sat there. Then my wife Dianne came in from the audience and asked, 'What's wrong?' As soon as I said it, I just broke down."

On the very same day that Wieland went down in a rain of Viet Cong gunfire, Norris's other brother, Aaron, was on a troop plane, en route to the same trouble spot. After Wieland was killed, the decision was made to transfer Aaron's duty assignment to Korea. Aaron wanted no part of this and applied for reassignment to combat duty in Nam time and again, but to no avail. His orders stood. "I just wanted to get there and bust some heads, kill people," he told *Spin.* "I had a real bad attitude after my brother was killed. I guess I came home a frustrated Vietnam veteran. I thought for a long time of becoming a mercenary."

Chuck was more philosophical. He had no real public vent for his feelings at the time of Wieland's death (although some of his former opponents have maintained that his fighting style became even fiercer in its wake), but he'd been hoping for an opportunity to pay homage to Wieland's memory ever since he got involved with films. In early 1983 he was finally offered a script that seemed to fit the bill. There was a slight hold-up, though. "When I went to Cannon for *Missing in Action,*" Norris told Truman, "they said, 'We've got a good MIA script.' And I said, 'So have I.' But I read theirs and it was good too. But so's mine. So we said, 'Well . . . let's do them both then.' That's how we wound up doing both. We shot them back to back."

Indeed, the two films form a definite (if unevenly matched) pair, even if the only character that makes an appearance in both is Norris's Colonel James Braddock. With the chronological dyslexia sometimes peculiar to the film industry, however, the film that was completed first and contained the kernel of the story was released after the other one. Thus, *Missing in Action* came out first, telling the story of Colonel Braddock's post-war return to Vietnam; then *Missing in Action 2: The Beginning,* telling the story of Braddock's activities during the war, was released. You figure it.

As *Missing in Action 2: The Beginning* opens, Colonel Braddock and his men are flying along in a chopper, deep behind enemy lines. They attract Viet Cong fire and are hit. The Huey crashes into the jungle below. North Vietnamese troops overrun the area and Braddock and the few surviving members of his platoon are rushed off to a prisoner of war camp. Unfortunately for them, this is not just any POW camp, but one that's a front for an international opium smuggling operation. It's run by a psychotic North Vietnamese renegade named Colonel Yin. Yin, who's completely off his rocker, enjoys torturing the men so much that he decides to keep them around even after the war ends and he's commanded to release them. It becomes Yin's personal obsession to get a phony confession to war crimes out of Braddock.

To achieve this goal, Yin uses every weapon available to him. With his enormous and brutal sidekick, Lao (played by Professor Toru Tanaka, also of *An Eye for an Eye*), Yin tries just about every imaginable torture on Braddock and his men. They are beaten, shocked, tempted, and told that their wives have taken lovers and remarried. Their dignity and self-respect is stripped away bit by bit through Yin's horrible machinations (he even goes so far as to strangle the chicken that one of the prisoners has taken for a pet). The foulest deed he visits upon Braddock involves a rat, a burlap bag, inversion boots, and Braddock's head (all in close proximity to each other). It is not a pretty sight. Finally, one day after the war is long over, a round-eyed stranger named Emerson arrives at Yin's end-of-the-world outpost.

Emerson is an Australian photographer who came to Vietnam to cover the war. After it was over, he remained in the country, photographing the debris that remained and the pathetic attempts the communists made to rebuild it. In the course of his travels he had heard rumors of Yin's camp and, after much searching, finally stumbled across it. He gains access to the fortress by telling Yin that he is the frontman for an official delegation that's searching for the remains of Americans still officially listed on the books as MIA. Even though he expected the worst, nothing could have prepared Emerson for the squalor he discovers in the camp. Sickened, he lets the men in on the fact that the war has been over for years, only to be beaten and executed when Yin discovers he's not on official business.

Soon after this, Yin at last succeeds in getting Braddock to sign a trumped-up confession by refusing to give quinine to one of the men who's contracted malaria. Knowing that his reluctance in putting his John Hancock on the paper will be directly responsible for the death of one of the men entrusted to his charge, Braddock finally gives in. Of course, once he signs, Yin proves his treacherous, lying nature in the most gruesome way possible. This is the event that finally causes Braddock to mobilize, and while *Missing in Action 2: The Beginning* may be a bit slow to get moving, it certainly has a bang-up last thirty minutes. Still, it's nowhere near as good as *Missing in Action,* which picks up Braddock's story after he's back in the States.

As *Missing in Action* opens, Braddock is lying in bed having a nightmare. He's reliving a battle from his Vietnam tour and after body covers body and Braddock lands on a hand grenade, he awakes in a cold sweat. The television is turned on in his room, and from it we learn that there will soon be a hearing in Ho Chi Minh City on the actual status of the 2,500 American troops still listed as missing. We also learn that Braddock is famous for having crawled out of the jungle, years after the war was over, claiming that he'd been held in a post-war POW camp. He maintains that other such camps still exist.

It's also said that Braddock has refused to offer any testimony for the hearings. Later, while he's idly watching a cartoon program showing Spider-man scaling prison walls and flag poles, another news blurb comes on about the MIAs. Braddock, a man of action, immediately kicks in the TV screen and gets on the phone to Washington. Regardless of his previous statements, he tells them, he would like to testify at the conference.

Getting off the plane at Ho Chi Minh City, Braddock sees that one of the chief North Vietnamese officials, General Tron, is the bastard who ran the camp in which he was held. In flashbacks, we've seen Tron torturing Braddock (in this film, Tron apparently stands in for Yin) and randomly executing Braddock's men. There is recognition of this in both men's eyes when they meet. The next day at the hearing Tron parades through the room a troupe of villagers who are supposed to have testified to the war crimes they saw Braddock commit. This attempt to tarnish Braddock's testimony is a pretty obvious scam on Tron's part and when Tron presses the point, asking Braddock why there was a $20,000 bounty on his head during the war Braddock coolly replies, "It was for killing assholes like you." Nice touch.

That night, under heavy guard by North Vietnamese intelligence and the military, Norris pulls a Spider-man of his own and goes on a stealthy tour of the town. He is able to get information on the location of the secret POW camp he's searching for without killing too many people and covers his tracks by getting romantically involved with one of the State Department emissaries with whom he's been traveling. Tron is not fooled, however, and Braddock is commanded to leave the country the next morning. He does, flying to Bangkok and hooking up with an old Army buddy named Tuck (played by M. Emmett Walsh, whose character has not aged quite so gracefully as Chuck's).

Braddock has been trailed to Thailand by Tron and some confederates, but he's used to dealing with that sort of problem. The rest of the movie deals with his and Tuck's two-man rescue mission. There are some wild action sequences featuring an assault raft that can go like a bat out of hell. The trouble Braddock and Tuck are able to stir up with their arsenal is damn impressive. It may be that Cannon knew what they were doing, after all, when they released this movie first. If *MIA 2: The Beginning* had been released first, it probably wouldn't have created the same kind of stir.

Interestingly, both films were shot under different titles from those under which they were released. *MIA 2,* directed by Lance Hool (previously noted as the producer of a trine of Charles Bronson films) and shot on location in Mexico and the tropical island of St. Kitts, was originally to be titled *Missing in Action. MIA,* filmed in the Philippines by Joseph Zito, was scheduled to be released as *Battle Rage,* over the protests of Norris who thought the title made it sound too much like a 1940s war epic. When the release schedules were shifted, so were the titles, and right up until the last moment, it looked like *MIA 2* would be called *Battle Rage.* Then Norris triumphed and, mere weeks before the film hit the theaters, the name was changed and everybody was happy. Well, almost everybody.

As usual, not quite all the critics were behind Norris's films. The Washington *Post,* a nemesis of long standing, said, "There's enough slow motion violence to make you wish that some enterprising congressman would introduce a bill forbidding the imitation of Sam Peckinpah." They went on to categorize Norris as "the poor man's Clint Eastwood" (recent adulatory coverage in *The New York Times* Sunday Magazine had seen to it that Eastwood was no longer the low-rent version of himself). Also *Variety* called *MIA* jingoistic and said it made *The Green Berets* look like mellow stuff. Presumably this was meant to be a jape.

The only other disgruntled folks this time around were some of Norris's original patrons in the martial-arts field. One complained that you could see more karate "in an average re-run of *Hawaii Five-O.*" Norris couldn't have cared less.

MIA took off like a rocket. The film raked in over $6 million during its first weekend and promptly rose to the number-one position. It did pretty well with a large section of the critical community as well.

People said, "While it is no *Citizen Kane,* it is Chuck Norris's best effort to date—an *Uncommon Valor* without the pretensions." Several other writers noted the film's thematic similarities to *Uncommon Valor* (a film released a few months earlier starring Gene Hackman, which had also dealt with the problems of Vietnam after the war), and Norris had this to say in the Houston *Post*: "Where *Uncommon Valor* didn't really deal with the MIAs, I do. I show the men with some character development. In *Uncommon Valor,* you didn't really have a feeling for the MIAs because you didn't get to know them. In this movie, when I do rescue them, there are moments you can feel the pain that these guys have gone through. I think that's what *Uncommon Valor* missed. And we didn't want to make the same mistake." He added that he had been closely involved with shaping the final version of the script and that the film "has a lot more than just action. It's a very dramatic type of film. *Lone Wolf McQuade* was the best film I'd done up to that time. But I think this is the best film I've done so far."

It was the message, however, that really set this film apart for Norris. "Since Vietnam I've really felt for the MIA families," he told the Los Angeles *Times.* "I mean, I lost a brother, but I know what happened to him. How about the other 2,500 who are missing? Their families don't know for sure that they're dead. That has to be a terrible and tragic thing to go through. Everything is so doggone negative. We didn't win the Vietnam War, and we didn't really get much out of it. But the fact is, Americans went over there and fought. What I did with *MIA* was to try and instill a positive attitude. What's wrong with that?"

"I was never in favor of the Vietnam War," he told Truman. "I do lay blame for expending lives in a situation where we couldn't win. We could have won the war in the very early stages if we had gone in to win it. But it was a political war and I hate political wars because they're fought to satisfy governments. That's what Vietnam was. We didn't go there to win the war, we went there to play around. Thousands of lives were lost because of those games. If you don't want to win the battle, don't get involved. We didn't have a will to win, but the Viet Cong did.

"The boys who came back from Vietnam were treated unjustly," he added. "I think people now realize that and feel bad about it and are trying to make it up. But I think the harm's been done. After ten years I think the vets are now finally getting the accolades they deserve. They should have come back as heroes. Although we didn't win the war, it wasn't their fault.

"Many of my characters have had to face the atrocities of Vietnam and come back and read-just their lives, like the college professor in *Good*

Guys Wear Black. MIA was a sort of tribute to all these men and it got a lot of response from the G.I.'s. This girl I met took her dad, a vet, to *MIA* and she said it was the first time she'd seen him cry. In all the years of growing up with her dad, that was the only time. It's amazing the emotion that does come out of some of my films. In some theaters we had standing ovations at the end of *MIA*. To see people standing up and giving your movie a standing ovation; that's what it's all about."

Well, maybe that's not what it's all about. It's also about box-office success, and the *MIA* films surely had that. At last report, their combined gross was in the neighborhood of $40 million and *MIA* was the top-grossing independent film of 1984. *MIA* was also noted as being one of the primary inspirations for Sylvester Stallone's hit, *Rambo*. That wasn't the only Norris film it pillaged for source material either. As *Spin* noted, *Rambo*'s plot was equal parts of *MIA* and *Good Guys Wear Black*.

When asked to comment on this by *The New York Times,* Norris replied, "I'm not quite so anti-government as Rambo is. When the helicopter comes to rescue Rambo and the American MIAs and then leaves them stranded—I found that unrealistic. There is not an American pilot alive who would leave them there. They'd have to shoot me to stop me from picking them up." On *Rambo*'s success, he added, "I'm just glad it's doing so well. It's expressive of the new spirit in America. I think Stallone's method or philosophy is similar to mine. It's the underdog overcoming the odds. It works. Fortunately for him, his budgets are huge, so he's able to get more on screen. That's what I'm working towards." And Norris is closing in.

10

Norris wasted no time in rushing through the doors that the *MIA* films' success opened for him. He was still contracted to do one more picture for Orion when *MIA* hit the streets, so he and a crack production crew (including twenty-seven stuntmen) sped through the making of *Code of Silence*. Directed by Andrew Davis (another protégé of Roger Corman) and shot throughout Chicago's grimy inner city in the dead of winter, it was the film that completed Norris's transformation into an actor with mainstream appeal.

Norris's role in *Code of Silence* (originally written with Clint Eastwood in mind) is that of Sergeant Eddie Cusack, a second-generation cop as tough and honest as they come. His father had been something of a local hero before he was cut down in the line of duty, and Cusack the younger feels obliged to keep the family profile high. To this end, he refrains from strong drink (very rare behavior for a movie cop) and even seems to be without a social life. About the only time we see him off the job, he's working out in a gym.

Code of Silence opens with a tremendous stakeout scene. Cusack, in the guise of a garbage man, is lingering under the elevated train tracks while his men infiltrate the area and a big drug bust is being set up by an informer. Before Cusack's men can close in on the Colombian coke hustlers, however, a bloody raid is launched by some soldiers of a local mobster named Tony Luna and the area is strewn with bodies. Among the dead are two brothers of the head of the Colombian mob, Luis Comacho (portrayed with psychotic fervor by veteran bad guy Henry Silva), who, while viewing the bodies at the morgue, promises their spirits that he will avenge them "blood for blood."

While at the morgue, Comacho runs into Cusack. Comacho takes real delight in telling Cusack how much he'd like to give him "a Colombian necktie" (cut his throat and pull the tongue out of the resulting wound). Cusack only smiles and says, "Yeah? Why don't you give it to me right here?" Comacho smolders off.

By the time we've gotten this far, there are also a number of sub-plots bouncing around. The first has to do with a lazy, alcoholic police-force veteran named Cragge. This creep shot an innocent kid down in cold blood and then planted a gun on him. His rookie partner, Nick, was witness to the whole sick act. Convincing him of the evil of squealing on a brother officer, Cragge has effectively gagged the rookie. Nick knows he's making a grave ethical error by not speaking up, but he feels trapped by the force's buddy-buddy system. The conflict is eating him alive.

Another undercurrent has to do with Anthony "Crazy Tony" Luna, who set up the hit on the Colombians apparently without asking his boss's permission. He is on everyone's hit list and has left town for a woodsy retreat. In his absence he's left a minion to watch after his daughter, Diane. It's through her that he reasons most parties would first try to reach him. The logic of this, unfortunately, proves to be faulty. Why? Because Comacho and Company are nuts.

While Cusack, saddled with Nick as a partner (Norris's characters never wear *compadres* well) for as long as Cragge's the subject of an investigation, does indeed follow Diane around Chicago in hopes of picking up a clue to her father's whereabouts, Comacho is not so circumspect. His men walk into Luna's family's house and kill everyone and everything that moves. Diane is only spared because she isn't at home.

When he learns of the clan's demise, Cusack rushes off in an attempt to spare Diane from whatever grisly end Comacho has planned for her. He gets to her place of work right on the heels of the Colombians. The sequence in which they chase her down a crowded Chicago street at midday is a potent comment on just how much violence city-goers will be happy to ignore in order to avoid involving themselves. Diane's goose appears to be cooked when Cusack appears on the scene. Luckily, Cusack has some patented methods for dealing with big, ornery, armed Colombians, and everything is soon under control. Cusack takes Diane to stay with a retired cop who was a good friend of his father's, then heads off to Cragge's hearing.

The only one telling the truth in the entire hearing room is Cusack. But when he informs the assembled crowd that in his opinion, Cragge is burnt out and shouldn't be on the streets, few applaud his candor. In the wake of this pronouncement, Cusack finds himself to be as popular as cirrhosis with his colleagues. They refuse to respond to his requests for backup when he goes to see Comacho and he's badly beaten by a Colombian horde as a result. On the way to defeat, however, he is able to deliver one heck of a classic line to one of his maulers: When a thug grabs his arm and says, "I don't think you want to be here," Cusack replies, "When I want your opinion I'll beat it out of you."

When Cusack goes to his next meeting with Comacho, he arrives well armed. His weapon of choice is called the Programmable Robot Observer With Logical Enemy Response (aka PROWLER). A real weapon, PROWLER can be equipped with microcomputers and sensors to identify intruders. It can also be equipped with a variety of weapons and programmed to fire of its own accord. For *Code of Silence* it's programmed to shoot a thousand rounds a minute and the battle utilizing it in a wharfside warehouse is really something.

Along the way to this climax, the viewer is treated to the funniest scene yet in a Norris film (two bungling robbers who try to hold up a bar that's a hangout for cops), some really beautiful cinematography by Frank Tidy (who did *The Duellists*), and much more. *Code of Silence* was every inch a winner, and this time there was almost unanimity in the critics' acclaim. Naturally, the Washington *Post* found nothing good to say. "Norris," they wrote, "has all the personality of a railroad tie." But they did sort of like the PROWLER, calling it "My Mother the Tank" (in homage to the speaking car that starred in Jerry Van Dyke's 1960s TV series). Most other periodicals gave the film much more positive notices.

"What's fascinating about *Code of Silence,* the much-praised Chuck Norris thriller (I agree with the praise), is the way it both imitates and criticizes Clint Eastwood's *Dirty Harry* series," wrote *New York.* "Norris here takes on Eastwood's patented role of ravaged urban avenger—the cop of 'unorthodox' methods and unlimited daring who stands alone in the police force. The difference in *Code of Silence* is that the enemy here is a corrupt, incompetent officer who not only threatens innocent people, but also makes it harder and more dangerous for everyone else to do his job. This may seem like an unexceptional piece of wisdom, but in a genre that recently has betrayed protofacist longings, it's almost a revelation. Two cheers for Mr. Norris. He might be appalled to find himself described as a pragmatic liberal, but he's tough enough to stand anything."

People called the movie "his most satisfying, exciting film," adding, "While Mr. Norris has always been bankable, now he's good and bankable."

The Gannet News Service was even more ebullient. "Move over, Eastwood," they crowed. "With *Code of Silence* Chuck Norris leaps into the number-one spot as today's most impressive action star. Norris, who stands four-square for action, plain and simple, delivers with fresh appeal. He's not only good at the rough stuff, but beneath the rough exterior beats a gentleness that makes it all the more effective when he destroys every enemy in sight."

Time pronounced that Norris "has become an undisputed superstar. Displaying tenacity and absolute cool, he is the first really bankable blond leading man since Robert Redford." *The New York Times* added that 'While *Code of Silence* is not *Little Caesar,* it stands at long last to put Mr. Norris up there with the other big guys of Hollywood law and order: Clint Eastwood and Charles Bronson. We are in the presence of a major 'new' movie star." And there was much more, all of it a far cry from the outright dismissal that had greeted so many of his early films.

Was Norris surprised by all the good press he got? "Yes and no," he told James Truman. "I thought *Code of Silence* was a very good film. I'd have felt bad if they knocked me. I've been in this business nine years, I've worked hard at it, and

I've become accomplished as an actor. I've tried to use some of the tidbits of advice that Steve McQueen gave me on how I should develop a character. I didn't do a lot of BS dialogue. Things like 'If I want your opinion I'll beat it out of you' you try to put in your films. Eastwood's a master at it. 'Make my day.' I'm not Dustin Hoffman. I don't like to do a lot of dialogue.

"One thing I'm very concerned with is the reality of my fight scenes," he went on. "And, in *Code of Silence* I didn't win. There were too many of them. No one's superhuman. You can be a good fighter, but you can only be so good unarmed. I don't mind losing, so long as I can get them back. Without that, the audience would be very disappointed. But in the end I do. I even the score.

"What I'm trying to do is movies that instill realism. If I've got a gun on my hip and I'm facing astronomical odds, it'd be a little ridiculous for me to get into a karate stance and fight. In order to be seen as a serious actor, you have to maintain a serious element in your films. I want my movies to be seen as action-adventures with karate scenes included if they're needed. I like doing the karate scenes, but I don't want to be pushing a square peg in a round hole and force karate in there where it's not appropriate. I've spent nine years trying to break away from the idea that all I do is chop socky. I'm finally breaking the mold. *Code of Silence* opened the door for me, but man, it's been a hard nut to crack.

"Karate worked well in *Missing in Action 2.* It

was very dramatic. The audience was rooting for me. That's what most kung-fu movies miss. I mean, there he is walking down the street when thirty bad guys circle him. He fights them and moves on. Then ten more. And you could really care less. If you want to see a little bit of technique, a few kicks, that's fine, but you don't really care. I want my audience to be involved, to feel what I'm feeling. I want them to cheer. When they do that I know I've achieved what I set out to do."

With *Code of Silence* there was no doubt that Norris had achieved what he'd been trying for all along. Besides receiving critical kudos galore, it also proved to be Norris's biggest box-office hit up to that point. It grossed almost $11 million during the first two weekends it was out and was number one on the box-office charts for a month. A hard act to follow? Definitely, but Norris has never been one to shrink at the thought of a challenge. The idea for his next film seemed like a sure winner.

The concept came to him one day while he was perusing the *Reader's Digest*. In it there was an article about three terrorist groups headquartered in Iran. Two of these groups were especially interesting to Norris, as their main goals were the furtherment of terrorist activities in the United States and France. The specific modus operandi of the organizations was to place operatives under what is called "deep cover." This means that they move to a country and operate as honest citizens for years or even decades until they're called upon by their superiors, at which time they go into action. Norris started thinking about the havoc they could wreak. What would the effect of this kind of terrorist attack be?

"The United States has gotten the reputation of being a paper tiger," he said in the film's press kit. "We must let other countries know that if they cross us they're going to have their hands full. I'm not really a hawk, but I think you need to take a firm stand and let others know where you are. This is patriotism and a lot of people have no time for it, but you and I know that until we get back behind our country, other nations won't respect us and we won't respect ourselves. In all the years I've been studying karate, I've never had to use it. But people know that if they push me, I'll push back."

In *Invasion USA*, Norris's character pushes back. Hard and fast. Cannon spared no expense helping him do so. "*Invasion USA* is the biggest budget I've ever had," Norris told Truman. "Cannon is not known for having loose purse strings, but they've given carte blanche with this movie. They're making movies with Roger Moore and Katharine Hepburn that are budgeted around five million dollars. What's great about them and why I signed a six-million-dollar deal with them is that they let me pick the director and the script." The director Norris chose was Joseph Zito, who co-wrote *Missing In Action*.

Invasion USA opens with a horrific scene. A boatload of refugees, apparently fugitives from

Castro's Cuba, meet a cabin cruiser on the high seas somewhere off the Florida coast (the refugees' declared destination). "Welcome to the United States," intones the boat's captain. The sailors open fire on the unarmed exiles, killing every man, woman, and child.

Less than one hundred nautical miles away, Norris's character, Matt Hunter, blithely wrestles with a crocodile near his Everglades retreat. Hunter is an anti-terrorist specialist who was once a member of the CIA. In this capacity, he was the only operative ever to thwart the nefarious schemes of the Soviet's villainous secret agent, Rostov.

In flashbacks we see how Hunter foiled one of Rostov's final capers and actually held Rostov's life in his hands. Holding a gun to the devious devil's head, Hunter chose to let Rostov live and he has regretted the decision ever since. Rostov managed to escape justice and has caused the ruination of untold lives since that time, including the massacre of the boat people. Hunter feels a certain responsibility.

For his part, Rostov has never forgiven Hunter for besting him in that long-ago battle of wits. His fondest dream is to see Hunter's bones picked clean by carrion birds. So while Hunter slogs through the swamps, Rostov enters the United States disguised as just another murderous ship captain.

Rostov's goal this time around is nothing less than to bring the United States to its knees. He has brought with him a large invasionary force of several hundred Communist mercenary-types. The CIA quickly figures out that something is up and, after learning that Rostov is behind it, they become desperate to have Hunter, their former top agent, come out of retirement. Various agents plead with Hunter to no avail, but the paranoiac madman Rostov soon launches a "retaliatory" attack on Hunter. Rostov only succeeds in icing Hunter's best friend and, after sending off his fallen pal with a funeral pyre that would have done the Vikings proud, our exspook has no choice but to rejoin forces with "The Company."

Hunter demands that he be allowed to work alone, without the encumbrance of partners. The Company contributes an amazing cache of weapons to Hunter, who blazes through the southeastern US in a gigantic off-the-road vehicle. He is equipped with a pair of tiny, amazingly powerful guns which are soon directed at the Russians, who have now landed in force.

It seems that Rostov (portrayed with an evil, lizardlike glow by Richard Lynch) has beached three landing crafts full of heavily-armed Russian agents. All hell breaks loose. Commies turn their bazookas towards defenseless Christmaseve tract homes, then dress up as cops and slaughter honest citizens. They blow up malls, dynamite churches, and generally cause mayhem and destruction. Eventually, martial law is imposed and the citizens cower in terror in their homes.

Hunter has been hot on Rostov's trail all

through this turmoil, and through some wily media manipulation he engineers a climactic showdown with the arch-villain near the top of Atlanta's towering Georgia Pacific skyscraper. Even though *Invasion USA*'s originally planned denouement—showing Rostov's flaming body falling 150 stories—was not used, the fiery battle between the two men is still an impressive showcase for the extra-powerful hand weapons currently available on the world market. In fact, many critics complained about this very aspect of *Invasion USA*—the use of a lot of high-powered automatic weaponry. Needless to say, the movie-going public had no such gripes.

In its first weekend, *Invasion USA* took in over $6.8 million, one of the biggest opening grosses ever reported for an American independent film. The film continued to draw moviegoers, making it the box office champion of the 1985 summer season.

The film's success was deserved. *Invasion* is a non-stop series of adrenalin-pumping climaxes. One scene blasts into the next like a bulldozer loaded with dynamite, pinning you to your seat.

Naturally, this sort of sensational slugathon did not offer the kind of coddling that critics crave. They sputtered violently from the windows of their ivory towers.

The Boston *Globe* was typical in its reaction, calling *Invasion* an exercise in "the unbelievable." *Newsweek* incorrectly pegged it as one of the "Sons of Rambo" (neatly putting the chicken before the egg). Most other critics followed suit and, indeed *Invasion*'s script did lack the subtlety of *Code of Silence*.

Still, *Invasion* was as solid and action-filled a movie as you could ask for, and several critics did review the film with Norris's intended audience in mind. After all, *Invasion* wasn't crafted for appreciation by an art theater full of aesthetes. The audiences who flocked to it were there to be entertained—and every time one of the bad guys bought it, theaters across America would erupt with shouts of glee. And since about ten guys were wasted every minute once the movie got into gear, theaters were raucous for *Invasion*'s entire length.

USA Today's review of the flick was right on the mark. That paper declared that "*Invasion* delivers for Norris fans." Man, does it ever. And, considering the constantly growing number of fans the guy has, that means it carries quite a wallop. Pow!

11

The question now becomes: What next for Chuck Norris? The answer is a simple one: At this stage of the game he can do just about anything he pleases. The only limits imposed on him are those of his imagination, and a mind which has conceived such films as *Silent Rage* is surely untroubled by any lack of feverish inspiration.

Norris's most recent action film, *Delta Force,* is his fourth feature for Cannon, originally planned to co-star Charles Bronson (an actor Norris has long admired and one to whom he has been frequently compared). By the time the Mideast production started filming, however, Bronson was out and two giants of the action-adventure genre—Lee Marvin and George Kennedy—were in.

"The story is very similar, due to a freakish coincidence, to the recent airport hostage situation in Beirut," Norris told *Moviegoer.* "But the script was written well before that occurred." In the film, Norris plays the leader of an anti-terrorist tactical squad that's called in when all other possibilities have been exhausted. It's a deucedly exciting picture in the style to which we've now become accustomed.

Asked by James Truman if he was interested in playing a new type of character, Norris shot back, "I like the type! I'm involved a lot in my films because I know what it is that I want to do. The whole thing is to find creative ways of dispatching characters. Like in *Invasion USA,* there's Rostov—the super bad guy. We have an encounter, we get to fighting, then he grabs a machine gun and I grab this flamethrower. We both fire, and I hit him right in the chest with this flamethrower. He goes flying out from a window 150 feet up, on fire. It's a beautiful shot with him falling 150 feet, on fire, past all this one-way mirrored glass that reflects him falling. All you try to do is think of creative ways to dispose of a bad element. Like at the end of *Missing in Action 2.* When I leave this guy and walk away, the audience is saying, 'Jeez, why did he leave him alive?' Then I blow him up and they go crazy. 'This is for me.'

"I go to all the theaters to see my movies," Norris continued. "I want to see what the audience likes and doesn't like, because my movies are made for them. They're the ones paying the money. They don't like me getting into sex scenes. They want me to be a free spirit, to be a loner—a guy who deals with whatever odds he has to encounter. I think the secret to the success of movies like mine is that people want someone to identify with. McQueen, Eastwood,

Bronson-type guys who are self-reliant, stand on their own two feet, and are not afraid to face adversity, give us something we all wish to do in real life. Movies are a way of releasing the youngster in us.

"I can have a romantic interest, like Barbara Carrera in *Lone Wolf McQuade,* but I'm not Richard Gere, where they expect me to do a very explicit love scene. I had that in *Silent Rage* and they didn't like it. What the audience wants to see is what I want to do. I'm not an emotional type. I don't go all to pieces thinking how I could have done better what I did before. When I see myself do something I don't like I just correct it in the future.

"It's my responsibility to give the audience the best that I can. Fantasy is what keeps life going. That's what's exciting—to entertain people to the utmost of my ability. That's what I aim to give an audience that comes to one of my films —entertainment. It's escapism, but that's what movies are—a way to get away and forget about the problems of everyday life. They still are that for me today. If I've got my mind on projects and future things and I want to block that out, I go to a movie.

"I don't like depressing movies, like *Terms of Endearment,* that deal with tragedies; they deal too much with reality in a close way. I don't mind movies, like *Invasion USA,* that deal with terrorism because it ends up being good in the end. But someone catching cancer and dying . . . you see that in real life. It's not the sort of thing you want to go to a movie for. I can't enjoy that.

"The worst thing that could happen to me now would be to hear someone leaving the cinema after seeing one of my movies, saying, 'Boy, did I get ripped off for my five bucks.' And that's important. If your movie is a box-office failure, no matter how much work you put into it or how great you think it is, you're in a world of trouble.

"One of the biggest thrills of my life came when I went to a theater in Westwood to see *Missing in Action.* When Colonel Braddock brought the POWs he's just released into a conference in Saigon where the politicians are saying there aren't any more prisoners of war, all the people stood up and applauded. Still, my motivation is more to entertain than to tell people something, even if, through the entertainment, a message does emerge.

"For instance, *Invasion USA* has the message that this could happen here, but it's also expressive of the new spirit of America. America is threatened to its foundations by terrorists and America fights back and overcomes them. It's the strong positive sense that we win in the end. We're threatened, we're pushed, we're beaten, but we win in the end. That's the American way. It's been that way for over 200 years.

"I'm very pro government—" a flag waver. What I like about Reagan is that he doesn't pussyfoot around. Like with Grenada. He went in there to take care of things and now it's reestablished, there's no problem. But he didn't play around. He went in there and he got the job done. And that's what you've got to do. You've got to be a strong president. You've got to make strong decisions that may not be in the wishes of whoever, but you're the one responsible. I'm not so much a Republican or Democrat. I go for the man himself. The thing about Reagan, the guy may stick his foot in his mouth occasionally, but he says what he feels. If you don't like it, that's just tough. I like that in a man. I don't like a man who says something because everyone expects him to say it. That's not the kind of leadership we need in our country. He can't be worrying about his popularity when our nation's at stake.

"There's a good example of this in our school system. First, they take out the flag. If kids don't pledge allegiance to the flag what gives them the spirit to be concerned about the flag—the symbol of our country? Nothing, and that's bad. Because that's your democratic patriotic sense of our country. Then there's the Lord's Prayer. They take that out of the school system because a small atheistic group says it's unconstitutional. So the majority suffers because a few people think it's unconstitutional. Well, they don't have to do it.

"What's happened is that the negative side of our country is winning over the positive side. All the things which are positive forces in our country are being eliminated. This is the thing that can ruin our country. I don't feel that Reagan lacks compassion for the underprivileged the way some people do. He just doesn't make a big hoop-de-doo about it. Other presidents have

said, 'Yeah, I'm for this.' But they don't do anything more than Reagan does. It's just that they
speak more. They speak, but they don't create
action. Now Reagan doesn't do a lot of talking,
he's not a bullshit artist, but I think he's done as
much for the underdog as any president. Our
economy's better than it's been in years and
years. The Carter years were disastrous. He was
always pitching for the underdog, but what did
he really do? You can always say things, but it's
the doing that counts. Because he doesn't talk a
lot about it, because he doesn't preach for the
underdog, a lot of people think he's not concerned. He's more action than words, and that
speaks for itself.

"You're always going to have poverty, the underprivileged, but you've got to cut it down as
much as you can. A lot of people just don't have
the drive, the will to succeed. To me, no one has
to be poor. I came out of a poor family. It's like
I tell kids today—whether you're in the ghetto of
Detroit or the backwoods of Oklahoma, you
have an opportunity in America. You travel to
any other country in the world and you won't
have the same opportunity. What you're born
with is where you stay, for the rest of your life.
In America you don't have to stay there. If you
don't have the drive, then you will. Nobody's
going to give it to you here in America.

"If I was Reagan, the kids that were heading
towards bad times or prison or both I would send
over to another country to see what other kids
are going through. Make them work there for X

amount of time. When they came back they'd have a whole new lease on life. That would be my prison for them. Send them somewhere where they would have to work and do good for somebody else in the world. At the same time they'd be seeing that they're not so bad off after all. I'm a nut about patriotism. If the United States declared war on another country I'd be right there at the front of the line. The best thing about having Reagan in office is that since he's been president there's been a more positive patriotic feel to the country." And there are few people more concerned with the positive than Norris. "The basic message has been the same in all my films: Just be the best that you can be."

"Basically, my characters do what they have to," Norris explained to the Los Angeles *Times*. "They resort to whatever they have to, to accomplish whatever it is they have to do. I try not to go to the extreme. I don't cross the boundary into ultra-violence. That's the fine line I have to walk, my cross to bear with these movies. One thing I've found is that the fight in the movie isn't as important as the buildup. There's got to be an emotional impact. You can't just have a fight for action's sake. The audience has to be pulling for you."

Asked by Truman whether it's become easier for him to rally the audience as he's gone along, Norris said, "Acting is harder now than it was nine years ago. As I become more accomplished as an actor I make more demands on myself. I learn from the audience's response what they like and dislike and build my films accordingly. In a screening room, I'm watching analytically; in a movie theater I just try to enjoy it.

"Making movies is like fighting—every time you do it you learn something new. That's why watching *Code of Silence* was so good. It was a fast-paced movie that didn't get bogged down in a lot of expositional dialogue. The audience got moved fast with a lot of emotion. To me movies should do just that—move. People should see the story visually, rather than hear it. A long time ago, Steve McQueen told me, 'If people can see it, you shouldn't have to say it.' I've learned to drop any lines that aren't important. Just watch Eastwood. He never speaks a word unless it's necessary.

"The hardest part of acting for me for a long time was the act of totally relaxing in front of a camera. After so many years of learning to control my emotions in karate, it was very difficult to reverse the process and fully express them. But I've developed more as an actor with each of my film roles and I've finally learned to do it. The scene in *Missing in Action 2* where the guy's being burned alive was the toughest I've done. I told the crew, 'This is a one-shot deal, guys.' To pull up all that emotion is very difficult. What I did was I didn't pull up past experiences, I put that person in my mind as being my brother—my brother being tortured. Immediately it brought up a very powerful emotion. I don't know how method actors can go back in their lives and pull up things. Maybe once, but after that surely the well is dry."

The acting isn't the only tough thing on a Norris set. For instance, Norris spent six on-location hours of *Invasion USA* deep in an Everglades mud holler wrestling an alligator. "I don't know who was more tired," he said, "the alligator or me. I like to do my own stunt work, but I'm not crazy. I'm not going to do something that might hurt me. I've done that already." Among his injuries, *People* counts a nose broken four times, a jaw broken once, and a shoulder broken twice. *The New York Times* adds an eighteen-inch scar over his eyebrow acquired when he fell out of a tree in *Missing in Action 2*. But the film Norris picked as the most personally grueling is *Missing in Action*.

First off, he got twelve stitches and a sixteen-inch scar just below his mouth from one scene. In another scene he received unexpectedly hard blows to one of his eyes. Also the overall tone of the film was so action-oriented—climbing buildings, jumping into moving trucks, leaping off high towers—that just keeping up with it was a project even though he says he's now stronger and faster than ever. (Exercise and positive thinking are the keys.)

Still, it's hard to imagine how even peak conditioning could have averted the most harrowing experience associated with *Missing in Action*. In the film's final scene, Norris was supposed to hang from the bottom rung of a ladder that a hovering helicopter would hold five feet over the surface of a lake. Norris got on just fine, and after a specified amount of time, the pilot of the chopper, believing Norris had gotten into the aircraft, took off towards the ocean. All while Norris was still on the end of the ladder! "It was up to 500 feet before I realized what was happening," he told the Houston *Post*. "And as I'm flying along, I go right over the cameraman, and even from up there I can hear him saying, 'Oh [expletive deleted]!' I'm looking down, wondering how long I can hold on. Finally, they radioed the helicopter pilot and told him I was hanging on. He turned around and dropped me on the beach. It was quite a scene."

Norris doesn't believe in keeping all the action to himself either. He's firmly dedicated to spreading the wealth. As he told the St. Louis *Post Dispatch*, "For *Silent Rage* we were going to use a double for Brian Libby in the last big fight scene, but Brian said he wanted to do it himself. He's in pretty good shape, but in the first shot I broke two of his ribs. He insisted on continuing and the next day he sprained his ankle. Also, in that movie's fight scene with the motorcycle gang, that was my brother Aaron who I hit in the stomach and then in the jaw, flipping him over backwards. When he landed, he hit his head and sprained his neck pretty good. He was used to it by then though. In *An Eye for an Eye* he'd hit his head on a window jamb going out a fourth-floor window, and that stunned him, so he landed wrong on the pad and broke a leg." And you thought the life of an associate producer (as Aaron has been billed for several films) was all glamour!

As it happens, Aaron, besides being the idea

man behind several Norris features, has also been the stunt coordinator for almost all of them. Aaron learned karate at an early age, and when he got back from Korea he and Chuck put together a touring martial-arts act. Wearing contrasting outfits, the brothers would grapple balletically to the beat of prerecorded music. They've been close collaborators ever since. Not surprisingly, Aaron also had a prestigious tournament fighting career and he's soon to follow the elder Norris's footsteps onto the big screen as well. He recently signed a three-picture deal with Armitage Productions and the first spawn of this match, called *The Deadly One*, will be unveiled shortly. A natural and easy-going actor, Aaron's would be a career to watch even if his brother were a nobody.

Also scheduled to get into "the picture" is Norris's oldest son, Mike. His first feature, *Arctic Heat*, a story of three college students winter-hiking in Finland who mistakenly cross over the border into Russia, is in the can, waiting for release. Other family members getting involved include Norris's younger son, Eric, who spends college breaks working as a double and gofer for whatever picture his dad currently has in the works. And it looks as if one picture that may be in the works before too long is an action-comedy called *City Slicker*, written by none other than Norris's wife, Dianne. Norris told *People* that she'd developed and nurtured the idea completely on her own and that he hoped to fit the movie into his schedule as soon as he feels confident enough in his career to start branching out.

Just where Dianne got the time to write *City Slicker* is not entirely clear, however. In 1983, with the boys well launched into the world, Dianne mentioned to Norris that she'd be interested in trying out the restaurant business. After looking around, the couple found a $600,000 place called Woody's Wharf that seemed to suit the bill. Located in Newport Beach, it was losing a reported $20,000 a month when they bought it. With typical Norris aplomb, Dianne has turned Woody's into the area's number-one restaurant, and that's to the credit of the whole family. Because no doubt about it, the Norris clan is one solid unit.

Maybe because of his own unhappy childhood or the spiritual resources opened up to him by the study of karate, the family unit has always been the most important thing to Norris. "With my kids, I just wanted them to know that I was there, that I cared," he told Truman. "I participated in a lot of their activities. I coached them in baseball for years. I was always at their high school games. I made a point that their friends didn't look at me as being an actor. So I'd have them come over to the house and we'd have hamburgers and all that stuff. If you see someone enough, then it's no big deal. I wanted the novelty to wear off."

Norris always stood up for his sons. "When Eric was in seventh grade there was this eighth-grader who was selling drugs," he recalled to *USA Today*. "He was also the school bully, so a lot of kids bought from him out of fear. He tried to force Eric to take a marijuana cigarette from him and they got into a fight. Eric worked him over pretty good"—both of Norris's sons have won karate titles of their own—"and forced him to eat the marijuana cigarette. The school called me in and said they were going to discipline Eric, but not the other kid. I said, 'No you're not. Whenever anybody tries to give my boys drugs they have permission to stick them anywhere they want.' " Later, Norris turned down an offer to do a film in Hong Kong because it meant he'd have to miss Eric's senior-year football season.

Family considerations are not the only reason Norris has given for turning down big roles. After he had inked his deal with Cannon Films, they worked hard trying to sell him on the merits of starring in *Death Wish 3* as a potential cross-over blockbuster. He declined the job (Charles Bronson has since decided to do it), saying that the script contained too much negative imagery and violence. "The character I want to build is a man who believes in the right things," he explained to *Time.* "A man who fights against drugs and evil."

Presumably to this end, Norris currently has several projects in various stages of evolution. There's a still-secret project to be filmed in Germany after *Delta Force,* a possible action-comedy about kick boxing. Wondering what a comedy vehicle for Norris might be like, Truman asked Norris what makes him laugh. "Well, people who bring out the light side in me." He said,

"I have a friend named Larry Morales who is a very jovial joke-telling type of character. Larry brings out the jovial side in me. He lightens me up. For comics, I like Joan Rivers, Abbott and Costello. I didn't like Chaplin, but I still watch Laurel and Hardy."

Asked about his favorite movies, Norris said, "Well, *Shane, Spartacus,* and *The Magnificent Seven* are the three that I've seen a dozen times or more. I always preferred the Western sheriff to Tarzan. I hope Westerns come back. Cannon doesn't seem to think they will. I asked them to do a Western but they didn't want to. I liked my Texas Ranger character in *Lone Wolf McQuade* quite a bit. Whether my audience would accept me in an 1880s-type role I don't know.

"The big question I always ask myself is whether I can make my next movie as successful as the one before. Can I do it again? The pressures build in different ways. First, you wonder if you can pay your bills. Then when you get to where you wanted to be, to where you're getting movie offers, then the pressures come in different ways. Are people going to like this movie? Am I doing the right movie? I feel I'm growing as an actor and eventually I would like to do something like *Raiders of the Lost Ark.*

"The thing you really have to watch out for is that you're not competing with or comparing yourself to other people. That's what a lot of actors do. 'Oh God. This guy's more successful than I am. Why? What can I do?' You really have to keep your life in perspective. An ego's an important thing, so long as it's a controlled ego. One of the main things that's changed with my life now is that it's not as easy to move around freely now. I enjoy meeting people, so it doesn't bother me. You do as much as you can to let them know you're not a snob, but obviously you can't do it for everybody."

Another change that's taken place, though, is the quality of the typical Norris fan, once described in the press as a simple wahoo with a taste for blood. "I got a letter from Burt Reynolds," Norris told Truman. "He was complimenting me on *Code of Silence.* He said he'd screened it for some friends at home and they all loved it. He said, 'The best compliment that I can give you is that I'm extremely jealous. Just remember—you're only as good as your last film, so be very careful with what films you pick. Love and respect, Burt Reynolds.' I thought, 'Gee. I've never even met the man.' For a man to take the time to write someone who's not even a peer. I thought it was really a class act." And over this last decade, Norris has become quite a class act himself.

"I guess I do like to keep busy," he recently told the Los Angeles *Times.* And when he asked, "What do you think? Am I making too many movies? Are people going to get tired of watching me?" you could almost hear all those "simple wahoos" in the background shouting a resounding "No!" "No!"

THE FILMS OF
CHUCK NORRIS

1) *The Wrecking Crew*
   (Columbia, 1968, 104 minutes)
   Not available on video
   Martial Arts Advisor: Bruce Lee
   Starring:
   Dean Martin
   Sharon Tate
   Elke Sommers
   Tina Louise
   Nancy Kwan
   Michael Green

2) *Student Teachers*
   (Americo, 1970, 79 minutes)
   Not available on video
   Director: Jonathon Kaplan
   Starring:
   Susan Damante
   Brooke Miller
   Bob Harris
   John Cramer
   Dick Miller
   Don Steele
   Robert Phillips
   Charles Dieskop

3) *Yellow-Faced Tiger*
   Re-released as *Slaughter in San Francisco*
   (Hong Kong, 1971, 87 minutes)
   Not available on video
   Director: William Lowe
   Starring:
     Don Wong
     Chuck Norris
     Sylvia Channing
     Robert Jones
     Dan Ivan

4) *Return of the Dragon* (R)
   (20th Century-Fox, 1973, 91 minutes)
   Available: 20th Century-Fox Video
   Producer: Raymond Chow
   Writer and Director: Bruce Lee
   Starring:
     Bruce Lee: Tang Lung
     Chuck Norris: Colt
     Wing Ping Ao: Ho
     Wang Chung Hsin: Way
     Nora Miao: Chen Ching Hua
     Robert Wall: Fred
     Wang Ing Sik: Japanese Fighter

5) *Breaker! Breaker!* (R)
   (Worldwide Distributors, 1977, 86 minutes)
   Available: Embassy Home Entertainment
   Producer and Director: Don Hulette
   Writer: Terry Chambers
   Starring:
     Chuck Norris: J.D. Dawes
     George Murdock: Judge Trimmings
     Terry O'Connor: Arlene
     Don Gentry: Sergeant Strode
     John DiFusco: Arney

Ron Cedillos: Deputy Boles
Michael Argenstein: Billy Dawes
Dave Vandegrift: Wilfred
Amelia Laurenson: Luana
The Great John L: The Polish Angel
Douglas Stevenson: Drake
Paul Kanecki: Wade
David Bezar: Tony
Deborah Shore: Pearl
Dee Cooper: Jailer

6) *Good Guys Wear Black* (PG)
   (Action One, 1977, 96 minutes)
   Available: Vestron Video
   Producer: Allan F. Bodoh
   Director: Ted Post
   Screenplay: Bruce Cohn and Mark Medoff
   Starring:
   Chuck Norris: John T. Booker
   James Franciscus: Conrad Morgan
   Lloyd Hanes: Murray Saunders
   Dana Andrews: Edgar Harolds
   Anne Archer: Margaret
   Jim Backus: Albert the doorman
   Larry Casey: Mike Potter
   Terry Mannino: Gordie Jones
   Soon Teck Oh: Major Mihn
   Aaron Norris: Al
   Joe Bennet: Lou Goldberg
   Jerry Douglas: Joe Walker
   Stack Pierce: Holly Washington
   Michael Payne: Mitch
   Don Pike: Hank

7) *A Force of One* (PG)
   (American Cinema, 1979, 91 minutes)
   Available: Media Home Entertainment Inc.

Producer: Alan Belkin
Director: Paul Aaron
Screenplay: Ernest Tidyman
Starring:
  Chuck Norris: Matt Logan
  Jennifer O'Neill: Mandy Rust
  Clu Gulager: Dunne
  Ron O'Neal: Rollins
  James Whitmore, Jr.: Moskowitz
  Clint Ritchie: Melrose
  Pepe Serna: Orlando
  Ray Vitte: Newton
  Taylor Lucher: Bishop
  Chu Chu Malave: Rudy
  Kevin Geer: Johnson
  Eugene Butler: Murphy
  Bill Wallace: Sparks
  Aaron Norris: Anderson
  Michael Norris: Pizza Skateboarder

8) *The Octagon* (R)
   (American Cinema, 1980, 103 minutes)
   Available: Media Home Entertainment
   Producer: Joel Freeman
   Director: Eric Kauson
   Screenplay: Leigh Chapman
   Starring:
     Chuck Norris: Scott James
     Lee Van Cleef: McCarn
     Art Hindle: A.J.
     Carol Bagsadarian: Aura
     Kim Lanford: Nancy
     Tadashi Yamashita: Seikura
     Kurt Grayson: Doggo
     Aaron Norris: Hatband
     Ken Gibbel: Meat
     Michael Norris: Scott at 18

Larry D. Mann: Tibor
John Fujioka: Isawa
Jack Carter: Sharky
Brian Libby: Deadwyler
Raymond Clarkson: Duffy

9) *An Eye for an Eye* (R)
    (Avco Embassy, 1981, 106 minutes)
    Available: Embassy Home Entertainment
    Producer: Frank Capra, Jr.
    Director: Steve Carver
    Screenplay: William Gray and James Bruner
    Starring:
      Chuck Norris: Sean Kane
      Christopher Lee: Morgan Canfield
      Richard Roundtree: Captain Stevens
      Matt Clark: Tom McCoy
      Mako: James
      Maggie Cooper: Heather Sullivan
      Rosalind Chao: Linda Chan
      Professor Toru Tanaka: Giant
      Stuart Pankin: Nicky Labelle
      Terry Kiser: Dave Pierce
      Mel Novak: Montoya
      Dorothy Dells: Taxi Driver
      Richard Prieto: Stark
      Sam Hiona: Ambler
      Don Pike: Watcher

10) *Silent Rage* (R)
    (Columbia, 1982, 100 minutes)
    Available: RCA/Columbia Home Video
    Producer: Anthony B. Unger
    Director: Michael Miller
    Written by Joseph Fraley
    Starring:
      Chuck Norris: Dan Stevens

Ron Silver: Dr. Tom Halman
Steve Keats: Dr. Phillip Spires
Toni Kalem: Allison Halman
William Finley: Dr. Paul Vaughn
Brian Libby: John Kirby
Steven Furst: Charlie
Stephanie Dunnam: Nancy Halman
Joyce Ingles: Mrs. Sims
Jay De Pland: Bike leader
Lillette Zoe Raley: Tattooed biker mama
Mike Johnson: Biker
Desmond Dhooge: Jimmy
John Barrett: Institute doctor
Russell Higgenbotham: Eddie Galt

11) *Forced Vengeance* (PG)
(MGM/UA, 1982, 103 minutes)
Available: MGM/UA Home Video
Producer: John A. Bennett
Director: James Fargo
Written by Franklin Thompson
Starring:
Chuck Norris: Josh Randall
Marie Louise Weller: Claire Bonner
Camilia Grigs: Joy Paschal
Michael Cavenaugh: Stan Raimondi
David Opatashi: Sam Paschal
Seiji Sakagucki: Kam
Frank Michael Liu: David Paschal
Bob Minor: Leroy Nicely
Lloyd King: Inspector Chan
Leigh Hamilton: Sally Tennant
Howard Caine: Milt Diamond
Robert Emhardt: Carl Gerlich
Roger Behrstock: Ron DiBiasi
Jimmy Shaw: Inspector Keck
Ken Argent: Danton Lord

12) *Lone Wolf McQuade* (PG)
    (Orion Pictures, 1982, 107 minutes)
    Available: Vestron Video
    Producers: Oram Ben-Ami and Steve Carver
    Director: Steve Carver
    Screenplay: B.J. Nelson
    Starring:
        Chuck Norris: James J. McQuade
        David Carradine: Rawley Wilkes
        Barbara Carrera: Lola Richardson
        Leon Isaac Kennedy: Jackson
        Robert Beltran: Kayo
        L.Q. Jones: Dakota
        Dana Kimmell: Sally
        R.G. Armstrong: T. Tyler
        Jorge Cervera Jr.: Jefe
        Sharon Farrell: Molly
        Daniel Frishman: Falcon
        William Sanderson: Snow
        John Anderson: Burnside
        Aaron Norris: Punk
        Oscar Hildago: Sergeant Garcia

13) *Missing in Action* (R)
    (Cannon Films, 1984, 101 minutes)
    Available: MGM/UA Home Video
    Producer: Lance Hool
    Director: Joseph Zito
    Screenplay: James Bruner
    Starring:
        Chuck Norris: Colonel James Thomas
            Braddock
        M. Emmet Walsh: Jack Tucker
        Lenore Kasdorf: Ann
        James Hong: General Tron
        David Tress: Senator Porter
        Pierrino Mascarino: Jacques

E. Erich Anderson: Massuci
Joseph Carberry: Carter
Avi Kleinverger: Dalton
Willy Williams: Randall
Bella Flores: Madame Pearl
Sabatino Fernandez: Dinh
Renato Morado: Mike
Jim Crumrie: Gibson
Jeff Mason: Barnes

14) *Missing in Action 2: The Beginning* (R)
(Cannon Films, 1985, 96 minutes)
Available: MGM/UA Home Video
Producers: Mehahem Golan and Yoram
   Globus
Director: Lance Hool
Written By Aurthur Silver and Larry
   Levinson and Steve Bing
Starring:
   Chuck Norris: Colonel James Braddock
   Soon Teck Oh: Colonel Yin
   Steven Willimas: Nester
   Bennett Ohta: Colonel H
   Cosie Costa: Mazilli
   Joe Michael Terry: Opelka
   John Wesley: Franklin
   David Chung: Dou Chou
   Professor Toru Tanaka: Lao
   John Otrin: Soldier
   Christopher Cary: Emerson
   Joseph Hieu: Guard
   Dean Ferrandini: Kittle
   Pierre Issot: Francois
   Mischa Hausserman: Kelly

15) *Code of Silence* (R)
(Orion Pictures, 1985, 100 minutes)

Available: Thorn/EMI/HBO Home Video
Producer: Raymond Wagner
Director: Andrew Davis
Screenplay: Michael Butler and Dennis
 Shryack
Starring:
 Chuck Norris: Sergeant Eddie Cusack
 Henry Silva: Luis Comacho
 Burt Remsen: Commander Page
 Mike Genovese: Tony Kuna
 Mervin Baylor: Tony Scialese
 Ralph Foody: Cragge
 Alan Hamilton: Perelli
 Ron Henriquez: Victor Cranshaw
 Joseph Guzaldo: Nick Caracas
 Molly Hagen: Diane Luna
 Don Pike: Hood on yacht
 Dennis Farina: Fenman
 Ron Dean: Arch

16) *Invasion USA* (R)
 (Cannon Films, 1985, 106 minutes)
 Available: MGM/UA Home Video
 Producers: Menahem Golan and Yoram
  Globus
 Director: Joseph Zito
 Screenplay: James Bruner and Chuck Norris
 Starring:
  Chuck Norris: Matt Hunter
  Richard Lynch: Rostov
  Melissa Prophet: McGuire
  Alexander Zale: Nikko
  Alex Colon: Tomas
  Eddie Jones: Cassidy
  Jon DeVries: Johnston
  James O'Sullivan: Harper
  Billy Drago: Mickey

Jaime Sanchez: Castillo
Dehl Berti: John Eagle
Stephen Markle: Flynn
Shane McCamey: Kurt
Martin Shakar: Adams
James Pax: Koyo

17) *The Delta Force*
(Cannon Films, 1986)
Producers: Menahem Golan and Yoram
    Globus
Director: Menahem Golan
Written by James Bruner and Menahem
    Golan
Starring:
    Chuck Norris
    Lee Marvin
    Martin Balsam
    Joey Bishop
    Kim Delaney
    Robert Forsterinie Kazan
    George Kennedy
    Hanna Schygulla
    Susan Strasberg
    Bo Svenson
    Robert Vaughn
    Shelley Winters

BOOKS BY CHUCK NORRIS:

1) *Winning Tournament Karate* (Ohara Publications, 1975, 130 pp., oversize paperback)
2) *Toughen Up!: The Chuck Norris Fitness System*
   (Bantam, 1983, 188 pp., oversize paperback)

Chuck Norris is also featured in the catalog from
Century Martial Arts Supply (1705 National

Blvd., Oklahoma City, OK 73110). The catalog has stills from his films, as well as action photos of him using the firm's equipment. The catalog costs $2 and an autographed picture is available also.